Samuel Wilberforce

The conflict of Christ in His church with spiritual wickedness in high places

sermons preached during the season of Lent

Samuel Wilberforce

The conflict of Christ in His church with spiritual wickedness in high places
sermons preached during the season of Lent

ISBN/EAN: 9783744745024

Printed in Europe, USA, Canada, Australia, Japan

Cover: Foto ©Lupo / pixelio.de

More available books at **www.hansebooks.com**

The Conflict of Christ in His Church with Spiritual Wickedness in High Places.

SERMONS

PREACHED DURING

THE SEASON OF LENT, 1866,

IN

OXFORD.

BY

The Lord Bishop of Oxford.
Rev. Professor Mansel.
Rev. J. R. Woodford, M.A.
The Dean of Canterbury.
Rev. Dr. Pusey.
Archdeacon Grant.

Rev. J. F. Mackarness, M.A.
Rev. T. T. Carter, M.A.
Rev. T. L. Claughton, M.A.
Rev. E. C. Wickham, M.A.
Rev. Dr. Payne Smith.
The Dean of Cork.

WITH A PREFACE

BY

SAMUEL, LORD BISHOP OF OXFORD.

Oxford,
AND 377, STRAND, LONDON:
JAMES PARKER AND CO.
1866.

Printed by James Parker and Co., Crown-yard, Oxford.

PREFACE.

ONCE again in this volume Sermons preached during Lent (1866) by preachers of my appointment are presented to the Church. The subject of these Sermons continues the series of last year. That series dealt with the struggle of the Church with the evils and corruptions around it in the world. This series traces up the conflict higher still; following it into the strife with those bands of spiritual beings whose existence, and many of whose actings, God's Word reveals to us. Greater interest than was ever manifested before, attached to these Sermons during their delivery. Once again it is my earnest prayer to God that by His grace He would make them effectual for His glory, and the good of souls.

S. OXON.

CUDDESDON PALACE,
    May, 1866.

CONTENTS.

SERMON I.
(p. 1.)
Our Spiritual Adversaries.
EPHESIANS vi. 12.
BY THE LORD BISHOP OF OXFORD.

SERMON II.
(p. 19.)
The Conflict and Defeat in Eden.
1 ST. JOHN iii. 8.
BY H. L. MANSEL, B.D.

SERMON III.
(p. 33.)
The Kingdom of Darkness Prevailing.
JOB i. 7.
BY J. R. WOODFORD, M.A.

SERMON IV.
(p. 47.)
The Coming in of the Son of Man.—His Conflict and Victory.
ST. JOHN xii. 31.
BY THE DEAN OF CANTERBURY.

SERMON V.

(p. 61.)

The Kingdom of Light set up.—The Conflict and Victory of its Faithful Children.

ST. LUKE xxiv. 49.

BY E. B. PUSEY, D.D.

SERMON VI.

(p. 81.)

The Powers of Darkness Prevailing over the Disobedient.

ST. JOHN iii. 19.

BY ARCHDEACON GRANT.

SERMON VII.

(p. 93.)

Aids in the Conflict:—God's Gifts of Grace.

HEBREWS iv. 16.

BY J. F. MACKARNESS, M.A.

SERMON VIII.

(p. 105.)

Aids in the Conflict:—God's Heavenly Host.

PSALM xci. 12.

BY T. T. CARTER, M.A.

SERMON IX.

(p. 123.)

The Communion of Saints.

ST. JOHN vi. 57.

BY T. L. CLAUGHTON, M.A.

SERMON X.

(p. 135.)

The Weapons of our Warfare.

2 Cor. x. 4; Rom. xii. 21.

By E. C. WICKHAM, M.A.

SERMON XI.

(p. 145.)

The Crisis of the Conflict.

St. John xvii. 3.

By R. PAYNE SMITH, D.D.

SERMON XII.

(p. 161.)

The Great Overthrow.

Psalm ix. 6.

By THE DEAN OF CORK.

SERMON I.

Our Spiritual Adversaries.

EPHESIANS vi. 12.

"For we wrestle not against flesh and blood, but against principalities, against powers, against the rulers of the darkness of this world, against spiritual wickedness in high places."

IN the course of Lenten Sermons which was preached last year in this place, we sought to set before you as many particulars as could be gathered within such limits, of the strife between Christ, in His Church, and the evil which is in this world.

This aspect of the conflict, even if it were complete in itself, would be but a partial and inadequate view of the whole mighty contention which through the ages is maintained between the Captain of our Salvation and the powers of evil. Not in this remote district of God's measureless kingdom—the battle-field though it be of an especial combat,—but not in it only or chiefly, is that warfare waged. Not with beings of our race only, the newest born, as it would seem, of the reasonable creation, did the strife begin; nor can we rightly understand its character, or duly measure its greatness, unless we take into our calculations those higher and earlier struggles, of which these in which we here bear part are the echo and the prolongation.

To set this, then, in some measure before you, is the object of this present course. We would shew you that not with flesh and blood alone is even here the struggle:

that around us, with us, through us, the mightier forms of more ancient wickedness are still maintaining their long warfare with the God of purity and love. Such a view of this present life, if we succeed in setting it at all duly before you, must be most full of practical suggestions. The greatness of our risk, the fierce and deadly character of the strife in which we must mingle, its past history, its present circumstances, its onslaughts and its helps, the weapons which must be wielded, the dark crisis yet to be encountered, and the measureless issues into which the final overthrow will run out through all eternity,—these, if they indeed sink into our hearts, must affect deeply our whole character, must add earnestness to our prayers, reality to our conceptions of the spiritual kingdom in which we are, and wariness, and courage, and undying resolution to the life we daily lead amidst such unseen but most present powers of good and of evil.

Our first enquiry in such a course must lead us to the questions who these, our enemies and God's, are; what is their nature; what the causes of their enmity to us; what the modes of their assaults, and the limits of their powers; questions, many of them doubtless difficult, some perhaps incapable of complete answer, and yet among them some greatly concerning us, which may have much light thrown upon them by reason, when informed and guided by revelation. It is as to these that I desire, by God's help, to speak to you to-night.

First, then, note the fact that there ARE spiritual beings, greater than ourselves in nature and power. To this the belief of man in all ages bears a remarkably consentient witness. The universal extent of this belief seems to base it upon the traditions of a primæval revelation. But even without such revelation, reason undoubtedly supports the view. For creation round us exhibits, wherever we examine it, an orderly gradation of existences. There are in all its vast extent no abrupt transitions. Inert matter is first raised into the shadowy vitality of vegetable life; thence, by links so subtle that we can scarcely ascertain the actual point of transition, it passes into the living animal; through the graduated series of irrational animal existence it mounts, by measurable steps, from the almost vegetable zoophyte up to the highly organized quadrumana. Then intervenes a measureless yet not unnatural transition into the reasonable creation, which we see and feel and know around ourselves. To suppose that here the series stopped abruptly, that between ourselves and the immaterial, self-existent, necessary Creator were interposed no higher order of created beings, would be to contradict all our precedent experience of the laws of gradation in His world. At this point, indeed, as at the transition from inanimate matter to animate being, and from irrational to rational life, the actual steps of the ascent are hidden from us, but our experience not only suggests to us that such steps exist, but, even further, indicate the direction in which they lead. We have already seen matter refined and exalted whenever the mystery of life, even in its lowest measure, is linked to it; we see it almost mastered by reason in man; and further, we see it in humanity knit into personal union with spirit, and so exalted, by the gifts to that humanity of reason and faith, that it can exercise a sovereign and wellnigh absolute command over all simpler elemental being. To conceive of it as carried on in higher creatures, into a far greater refinement, and endowed in them with a proportionate increase of power, is but to follow the intimations given clearly by the past. Moreover, the same experience leads us to expect that amongst these higher beings we should find the most intense variance in moral character. For if the denizens of that spirit-world exhibit in themselves the prolongation of the lines of being which are round us now, this divergence with which we are so familiar here must widen almost infinitely there.

So much we might reasonably look for from our actual knowledge. And at the point where the lack of experience stays the further enquiries of reason, revelation comes in and takes up in clearer tones its faltering accents. It tells us that there are in God's world all these expected gradations of existences; that ten thousand times ten thousand angels carry up the interrupted chain of reasonable personalities from men through all the ranks of shining ones, through spirits, dominations and thrones, through cherubim and seraphim, through angels and archangels, up to those created beings who stand nearest to the still unapproachable Jehovah. Further, it tells us distinctly of a mighty moral variance amongst these forms of power; of angels which kept not their first estate, who through choosing sin instead of God lost the blessedness for which they were created; whose marred proportions exhibit, even through their remaining majesty and power, the blackness of rebellion and the thunder-stricken scars of righteous vengeance. These fallen ones revelation pourtrays to us as a countless multitude, which, like the hosts of light, exhibit all gradations of power; which have gathered round one mightier than themselves in evil, and having rebelled against the God of light, yield themselves to the evil will of the prince of darkness. Over against the King of Heaven, and the hosts of His spirits of glory, scowl in vanquished, yet hating defiance, the devil and his angels;

who are further shewn to us in active opposition to the will of God. Here, then, the conflict, as we see and know it in this world, is distinctly revealed to us as existing in this higher region above us. The battle of the earth is the shadow and the echo of the strife on high.

But, beyond this, God's Word distinctly tells us, in a multitude of passages, that the evil spirits take a present and active part in our own conflict. "Your adversary the devil, as a roaring lion, walketh about, seeking whom he may devour[a]." To such a degree, indeed, is this true, that our conflict, as it is spoken of in Scripture, becomes a struggle against these evil ones. "Resist the devil, and he will flee from you[b];" "Neither give place to the devil[c];" "That ye may be able to stand against the wiles of the devil[d];" "Lest he fall into the snare of the devil[e]." This is the very description of our conflict, and pre-eminently in this verse which I have already read to you, does this great spiritual fact come out with a really terrible clearness. "Be strong," says the Apostle, "in the Lord, and in the power of His might. Put on the whole armour of God, that ye may be able to stand against the wiles of the devil. For we wrestle not against flesh and blood, but against principalities, against powers, against the rulers of the darkness of this world, against spiritual wickedness in high places." Every word is emphatic. The more emphatic as you look the closer into them. The wrestling, the πάλη, is the close, deathlike struggle; the limb to limb, the muscle to muscle embrace of agonizing strife; the whole man, the whole devil, is in that desperate anguish of encounter. And this is the very heart of our conflict;

[a] 1 St. Pet. v. 8.   [b] St. James iv. 7.   [c] Ephes. iv. 27.
[d] Ephes. vi. 11.   [e] 1 Tim. iii. 7.

it is not only πάλη, but ἡ πάλη, *the* wrestling, as if it were the only struggle worth the name.

Mark, too, that it is not said that our wrestling is not *only* with flesh and blood, but absolutely, that *it is not* with them. They disappear, as it were, from the sight of the purged eye, for they are but the weapons and the instruments of the mightier enemy; "they are vessels, another uses them; they are organs, another handles them." And fearful is the description of these greater foes. They are so many that they fill the air over us, seeking to cut us off from God. They are spiritual armies of wickedness, not limited, as we are, to this lower earth, but piled up in their subtle essences we know not to what extent, throughout this whole universe. And, fallen as they are, their might is great. They are τὰς ἀρχὰς, τὰς ἐξουσίας, τοὺς κοσμοκράτορας, —the governments, the powers, the world-rulers, in this time of its darkness. Which description involves a deeply mysterious subject, but one not to be passed wholly over; I mean, in what sense it is that these Evil ones are spoken of as world-rulers in this world of our God. In many passages of the New Testament the idea re-appears. The devil is "the prince of the power of the air, the spirit that now worketh in the children of disobedience f." In the record of our Lord's temptation in the wilderness, a wonderful aspect of the same spiritual fact is set before us, when the Evil One asserts, "All this power will I give THEE, and the glory of these kingdoms of the world: for that is delivered unto me; and to whomsoever I will I give it." For simply to deny his power of doing that which he offers to do, is to empty the temptation of that reality which the Word of God plainly attributes to it. For if it

---

f Ephes. ii. 2.

were a simple lie, how could it try the fidelity of the Incarnate Son? No doubt it did address itself to the nature He had assumed into oneness with the Godhead. No doubt it was a suggestion that man might, by the co-operation of the enemy, be redeemed without the Cross; that humanity might be delivered by the Son of Man receiving from the God of this world what he would yield voluntarily, so only that it should be held of him. It is hard for us, from the centre of Christendom, to see to how great a degree the boast was then literally true. It is only as we thoroughly remember what the old heathendom was, with its lust and its blood, its oracles, its idolatry, and its atheism, that we can see how much it was indeed the kingdom of the prince of darkness. As we muse on these things, we can see the dark forms of the Philistine host crowning every hill-top, and filling every valley with their array, before the arm of God had driven them out and cleared the land for the dwelling of His elect. The claim to dominion, moreover, which was thus asserted by the Tempter, agrees with our Lord's own thrice [g] repeated designation of him as "the prince of this world." Whether that title refer only to the dominion he establishes over those who, leaving God's side, join themselves to the great rebel, and become his slaves; or whether, beside and beyond this, it implies, as so many of the wisest have gathered, that in the economy of God's wide government this earth had been, before the great archangel fell, the special place of his vice-royalty, from which he is not yet cast absolutely out, it is perhaps impossible for us to say. It may well be so: and if it be, what a terrible force does it give to the picture of this wrestling of ours with this fallen, but not yet altogether subjugated power.

[g] St. John xii. 31, xiv. 30, xvi. 11.

Nor is this all; for the same thought throws much light also on the causes of the bitter hatred to us of these spirits of evil; and the terror of contest is increased by the extremity of their malignity with whom we have to strive. Doubtless they hated man in his innocence, because he was innocent; as impurity always hates purity; as unbelief hates faith; as the evil ones hate God and the holy angels; and so, raging against holiness, they desired to destroy its existence in God's creature. The Enemy "was a murderer from the beginning," because "he abode not in the truth [b]." But beyond this: if, as seems to be intimated in the Word of God, man was created to fill the places left void in the heavenly hierarchy by the angels' fall; if he was planted here as God's new vicegerent over all the new creation of this world, then there were added fresh reasons for the special hatred of the fallen angel to the race which had supplanted him in this his old dominion [l]. Thus, too, it followed that the rebellion of the new viceroy restored to a great degree the old dominion of the accursed one. For, in Adam, man yielded up his own commission and went over to the side of the enemy.

And so we may pass naturally on to see how these enemies can now assault us; and this sight, again, will add to the terror of the conflict. For though, doubtless, their uttermost malignity is restrained by God's over-mastering hand, yet have they still, as the very titles of "principalities, and powers, and world-rulers" intimate, a mighty remaining sway. And first, plainly, they can suggest evil in alluring forms to our apprehensions. Satan could put it into the heart of Judas to betray his Lord. He could "fill the hearts of Ananias and Sap-

[b] St. John viii. 44.   [l] "Diabolus cadens, stanti invidet."—*S. Aug.*, tom. vi. 992, 6.

phira to lie unto the Holy Ghost[k]." He could desire to have St. Peter, and actually did lead him into circumstances of temptation which were too strong for him, and then infuse into his mind the sudden thought of shame and fear under the sway of which his mighty spirit fainted. The subtle essences of these enemies, their intellectual vigour, their unperceived presence, their close neighbourhood, their spiritual powers, all doubtless enable them to suggest with their poisonous whisper to the too receptive spirit of fallen man, the pleasantness of a sensual indulgence, or the boldness of an unbelieving scoff, or the falsehood of a convenient lie, or the cowardice of an unlawful compliance, or assent to an angry feeling, or the treason of harboured and encouraged doubt. These are the fiery darts they can cast into the too open soul. Amidst their special powers seems to be that of presenting the φαντασία of pleasure, of fear, and the like, before the mind, and so acting upon the lower faculty of the fancy as to mislead the higher spiritual mind. And as any one yields to them, their power increases. He passes from under the pierced Hand which has been sheltering him; he goes forth from the tent of God's guarded ones to see the daughters of the land, and the enemies crowd round him as in the daring of his folly he wanders idly into their abodes; and be he never so strong he is close to an overthrow. He sleeps upon the knees of his Delilah while there are lyers in wait in the chamber of whom he never dreams, and his locks are shorn by some carnal indulgence; and at once the Philistines, who trembled before the champion of the Lord, are upon him, and when he would go forth as at other times, lo, the strength of the Nazarite has departed from him.

[k] Acts v. 3.

Upon such an one the enemies crowd in; sensual, impure, dark, unbelieving imaginations multiply upon him like the swarms of flies in the plague-time of Egypt, until the very dust which floats in the air breeds them in countless multitude, and he cannot escape; he has invited the enemies and they are come. It is an awful end. Perhaps we may find its clearest exhibition in the miserable demoniac, in whom the devil has been suffered to seize upon the bodily organs of his slave and make them do his evil bidding. Wonderful, as we gaze into it, is that miserable state; two personalities, in their tangled windings, seem inextricably interwoven; the consciousness of the man still lingering on in the midst of his vanquished self-command; his vain struggles to withhold the use of his bodily organs from the grasp of the overruling hand; the trouble of his astonished mind, now scarcely knowing which is his own utterance, which the devil's; the dark, inner whirlwind which hurries him on, casting him into the fire and into the water; which leads him to blaspheme when a faintly struggling desire of freedom would make him pray; which forces him into closer and yet closer union with one whom, because he is not himself a devil, he must hate, and yet from whom, because he has yielded himself up to him, he can no more escape—here, indeed, we may see what, even as to the body, is the fruit of opening the soul to the suggestions of the adversary. Nor ought we, I believe, to confine the power of our enemies merely to these secret suggestions to our spirits. Cunning men can so arrange circumstances as to bring about their own plans without in the least degree trenching upon the entire freewill of others. Why, with their wider experience, should not these craftier spirits do the like? How, otherwise than by such power over circumstance, could Satan once and again have hindered[1] St. Paul visiting his Thessalonian converts? In many ways this working of the Evil One becomes almost palpable. For does he not suggest to one the evil thoughts and deeds which make him the tempter and destroyer of another? How often does there leave some holy home a young man, nurtured carefully, and with all the bloom of early promise rich upon him. He comes up, it may be, to this very place. He is thrown, as we say, into bad company; the enemy, doubtless, is permitted to assail him in order to test and mature his better principles, thereupon the Evil One stirs up to a flame the sinful hearts of those who are already his victims. The new comer is attractive; he is worth the winning; iniquity puts forth all its powers of pleasing in order to seduce him; he is led into unwatchfulness; into sinful indulgence; into vice of some sort or another; his innocence is lost; step by step he is lured on by his visible tempters, who are doing the evil work of the invisible Enemy. It may be, the work is done thoroughly. The pure soul is soiled; sin has eaten deep into the life of one more redeemed man; he has become fit to be the tempter of others; and so the race of those who learn to serve evil, and at last, to hate God, is handed on amongst us through generations of iniquity. Surely, if human craft, with fitting instruments, can hold the skein of wicked counsel with so discerning an intelligence and successful a hand,—the numbers, the might, the cunning, and the hatred of the Evil ones must give them tenfold power against those who yield to them. If *we* can, by science and by art, obtain such a mastery over the elements around us, why should not *their* greater capacities, and wider ex-

---

[1] 1 Thess. ii. 18.

perience, enable them, with no power of working real miracles, yet to practise lying wonders; and with no power of altering the uniform acting of the laws of nature, yet to vent their hatred in stirring up the storm from the wilderness which smites the four corners [m] of the reveller's house, which guides the lightning's shaft to the frightened flock, or sinks beneath the waves the doomed ship? It is not, I believe, possible for us to ascertain absolutely the bounds which God has fixed to their exerting these powers of working harm. Such passages as that in which St. Paul speaks of the thorn in his own flesh as the messenger of Satan, surely implies that the limits are wide. Perhaps they are left uncertain to teach us, on the one hand, the difficult lesson of perpetual watchfulness; to make us feel the blessedness of being always under the shelter of the Cross of Christ; perhaps, on the other, we are not suffered to know all, lest it should drive some of us to cower before the foe, and lose all in absolute despair.

Enough is told us for our instruction. Certainly these enemies can approach our souls; if their power be now restrained from directly harming with their evil works the bodies which Christ has redeemed, and which have been signed with His Cross, they can, through our souls, seduce us into excess, debauchery, sensuality, and drunkenness, and so work out their full purposes of hatred even against the bodies of those who yield to them. Of how many bodily sufferings might this exercise of their power be seen to be the cause, if the hidden secrets of all lives were disclosed! How many a man bears with him, through a saddened life to a painful death, the bitter memorial of early sin! How often, and often, is it still the history of such transgressions and their

[m] Job i. 19.

punishment, that the suffering man is groaning under the evil inheritance of the sins of his youth! Of how many sufferers might He who reads all hearts still say, "Whom Satan hath bound, lo, these eighteen years [n]!"

One other mode in which the devil's hatred acts against us is too clearly revealed to be passed over, though the subject may be too mysterious for our full comprehension. Satan not only stirs up man against God, but he seeks in his malignity to stir up God against us. He is "the accuser of our brethren, which accused them before our God day and night [o]." So we read that he accused Job before his Maker: "Doth Job serve God for nought [p]?" From which words of Holy Writ it would seem as if all along the course of the conflict, which is to be ended by the utter overthrow of the enemy, he appeals to the justice of the All Just against the new race. The Evil One cannot comprehend good; he notes all our sins, marks all our haltings. In his keen envy he searches out our every failing. "Diabolus," says St. Augustin, "omnia nostra peccata rimatur diligentiâ invidentiæ [q]." He cannot appreciate the struggles of that blessed principle of faith which God sees in the weakest believer; the all-hating cannot bear, as can the infinite sympathy of Christ, with the infirmities of the elect; and so in his rage he cries even to our God to vindicate His justice by the destruction of the fallen though redeemed creation.

Here then, brethren, is this mighty conflict, now that we have followed it into the world of spirits. Here are our adversaries, in their nature, number, hatred, power, and means of assault. Surely the practical lessons which such a sight should teach lie open before us.

[n] St. Luke xiii. 16.   [o] Rev. xii. 10.   [p] Job i. 9.
[q] St. Aug., tom. vii. 820, d.

I. How great must be the severity of such a conflict! Can you not, as you gaze upon it, enter more into the depths of the Apostle's meaning, when he says that this, our death-struggle, is not "against flesh and blood, but against principalities and powers?" And as time advances there is doubtless increased vehemence in his assaults, and augmented subtlety in his wiles. Ages of experience have taught him every weakness and winding of the heart of man. More or less he has succeeded in harming every one born of woman save the King of Saints. His temptations, as might be expected, grow in subtlety as his experience ripens. The dangers of these present times bear all the marks of his perfected cunning and enduring malignity. As his short-lived triumph draws nearer, we may look to see more and more of the perfection of his work of evil. And this conflict every one who lives to the perfect development of his reason must pass through. It cannot be escaped. By day and by night, in company and alone, in the world and in church, in your business and on your knees, the adversary is beside you, to resist, and if he can prevail, to destroy you. Specially should this thought guard us against secret sins, against the impurity, the anger, the sullenness in which we are tempted to indulge when, as we think, no eye is on us, no one marking us. Then, in that lonely chamber, if the darkness revealed him, you might see the Evil One close beside you, working his will upon you; you might see the light which floated round your angel guardian passing, as you drove him from you, into the blackness which is round about the enemy. Oh, trifle not with such perils; oh, slumber not upon your watch; oh, yield not, for to yield is destruction; oh, "resist the devil, and he shall flee from you."

For, II. none can resist to the end, as Christ's soldiers, and not conquer.

The strongest of these enemies is God's creature. "Diabolus," says the great Augustin, "nihil facit, nihil potest, nisi missus aut permissus ʳ." The Almighty Will suffers them to be; to tempt, to harass, to vex us for purposes of His own love and wisdom, which one day we shall understand, as we cannot now. We can, indeed, now see that temptation is overruled so as to be God's instrument for our sanctification. "Diaboli tentationes," again says St. Augustin; "ad utilitatem sanctorum convertit Deus ˢ;" "Diabolo utitur Deus ad salutem fidelium ᵗ;" "Diabolus affligendo exercet non nocet: sæviendo prodest ad coronam ᵘ." Thus Satan is ever outwitting himself; by afflicting he trains us, by raging against us he secures and brightens the crown of which he would rob us. "Happy is the man that gets to heaven at last, though the devil himself hath a hand unwillingly in driving him thither." It is a noble expression of the holy apostolic bishop and martyr Ignatius to this purpose, in his Epistle to the Romans: "Let the punishment, stripes (κόλασις) of the devil come upon me, provided only I may obtain Jesus Christ ˣ." But we may go even beyond this; we may see that it is God's high will that the enemy should be cast down not by mere force, but by moral conquest. And this we may well believe is shewn specially to all the reasonable creation when the justice of God is vindicated against the false accuser by the faith and obedience of the saints. Their very weakness exalts their victory and the triumph of God's grace in them. And thus, therefore, do the saints conquer, not by any other might than by

---

ʳ St. Aug. iv. 456, d.   ˢ Ibid., tom. ix. 374, b.   ᵗ Ibid., tom. ii. 87, a.
ᵘ Ibid., 185, c.   ˣ Bishop Bull's Sermon "On the Holy Angels."

"the blood of the Lamb, and by the word of their testimony, and by not loving their life unto the death y." Rejoice, then, thou tempted one, even in the sight of this champion of the evil host. God's honour is at stake in thy overcoming; the sling and the stone shall yet bring down the uncircumcised Philistine. Thy Lord, in thy nature, met the Evil One in all his power, and overcame him utterly; and He shall bruise Satan under thy feet shortly.

Only, III. see that you fight as His servant. Fight in His Church, under the shadow of His Cross; claim and hold thy place in the host over which floats evermore that blood-red standard. Go not out of it, lest thou deliver thyself unto Satan. Remember that though he is no ruler in Christ's regenerate world, he is yet the ruler of the darkness of this world. Walk, then, in the light, with the children of the light. Forsake not the assembling of yourselves together; hold fast the form of sound words; keep within the new Jerusalem. Let not the host of the uncircumcised find thee wandering, for idleness or vaunt, or curiosity or lust, into the land of the Philistines; hold thyself, for thy safety, in the city of thy God. There is the great Captain of thy salvation; there are the sacraments of His grace; there the prayers and blessings, and examples, and fellowship of His elect; there the fiery squadrons of His unseen army filling the mountain round about His prophet. Abide thou there, and be faithful in thy post, and thou art safe for ever. But do thy own work in that thy post. Take unto thee all the armour of God; mortify thy lusts; use thy Lenten aids of prayer, watching, and fasting with Christ. Remember the Master's word: "This kind goeth not out but by

y Rev. xii. 11.

prayer and fasting[a]." A life of sloth, or ease, or indulgence, is not His life. Follow Him indeed, and the enemy shall not harm thee. His grace shall not fail thee, His love shall not forget thee, His arm shall not cease to shelter thee. He is at thy right hand, thou shalt not be moved. Yea, and soon thou shalt see the blessed end. The tarrying ages have almost passed; the eastern sky burns beneath the coming footsteps; the army of the saints is massing; this very Easter may, for aught we know, see the Lord amongst us in all His manifested glory. And then comes the mighty overthrow; then shall the accuser be cast down; then, beside the Master, shalt thou judge angels; then shall be the victory which thou hast expected; then shall the dark forms for ever vanish from thine eyes; then shall evil, driven in upon itself, be for thee a terror of the night that is over, remembered only to exalt the triumph of His might and of His love, who hath by the blood of His Cross lifted thee above it. Then shalt thou have reached the bright, the blessed, the eternal rest; when He hath "put all enemies under His feet[a]," and when, through His almighty grace, for each one who hath endured unto the end, "this corruptible shall have put on incorruption, and this mortal shall have put on immortality, and death shall be swallowed up in victory."

[a] St. Matt. xvii. 21.   [a] 1 Cor. xv. 25.

SERMON II.

The Conflict and Defeat in Eden.

---

1 ST. JOHN iii. 8.

"*He that committeth sin is of the devil; for the devil sinneth from the beginning.*"

VERY simple, yet very sublime in their simplicity, are the words which commence the record of the creation of the visible world: "In the beginning God created the heaven and the earth. And the earth was without form and void; and darkness was upon the face of the deep. And the Spirit of God moved upon the face of the waters. And God said, Let there be light: and there was light." Yet how much is the import of these words enhanced, even beyond the sublimity of their first and most obvious signification, when we come to elicit the deeper and more secret meaning which lies hidden under that pregnant sentence, "The earth was without form and void;" and interpret it according to the meaning suggested by the only two other passages of Holy Scripture in which the same expressions occur. When Isaiah, foretelling the future destruction of the land of God's enemies, declares, (using in the original the very words of Genesis,) "He shall stretch out upon it the line of confusion, and the stones (or rather, the plummet) of emptiness[a]?" or when, still more closely, Jeremiah, foreseeing the approaching desolation of his own country, announces his vision in

[a] Isaiah xxxiv. 11.

the words, "I beheld the earth, and lo, it was without form and void [b]," our thoughts naturally revert to the language which describes the chaos preceding the six days of creation; and we learn to interpret this also as indicating the effect of destruction, not the condition of formation; not as asserting, what indeed of itself it would be hard to believe, that confusion and emptiness was the primitive state of the world under the first effort of its Maker's hand, still less as lapsing into the heathen dream of a chaotic matter, moulded and formed, but not created, by the Almighty Mind; but as telling us, briefly and obscurely, yet not the less certainly, of God's power to destroy as well as to create; as pointing dimly and darkly to that whose details concern not us as a lesson of religion, and therefore have not been revealed to us,—that interval, how long we know not and how occupied we know not, from "the Beginning," when finite existence first came into being and the successive moments of time first broke forth from the unchanging *now* of eternity, to the day when He who made all things very good, was pleased for His own good purposes to bring destruction upon His own work; and then once more to renew it as a habitation for the children of men.

As it is with the natural, so it is with the moral world: the record of man's fall runs parallel with the record of his creation. The history of the six days' work closes with the words, "And God saw every thing that He had made, and, behold, it was very good:" the history of the temptation begins, "Now the serpent was more subtle than any beast of the field which the Lord God had made." Whence came this evil subtlety into

[b] Jeremiah iv. 23. See Pusey's Lectures on Daniel, Preface, p. xix.

a world which God had made very good, even, as we read, down to "every thing that creepeth upon the earth?" Here again there is a blank between—a blank whose solemn silence is more eloquent than speech, pointing darkly and dimly to another mystery of destruction, to something which came not in the beginning from the hand of God, but which came nevertheless, we know not when, and we know not how. If we turn to other passages of Scripture, the mystery is not explained—probably to our present faculties it could not be explained—it is but thrust back to a yet earlier world, and to beings of a nature different from ours. We read of "that old serpent, called the Devil, and Satan, which deceiveth the whole world," and of "his angels," who are "cast out with him[c];" we read, in the words of my text, that "the devil sinneth from the beginning," and again, that "he was a murderer from the beginning[d];" yet, as if expressly to confine these words within the boundaries of finite time, to preclude the possibility of any Manichean fiction of an evil power coeternal with good, we read also of "the angels which kept not their first estate[e];" we are told that "God spared not the angels that sinned, but cast them down to hell, and delivered them into chains of darkness, to be reserved unto judgment[f]." The mystery of iniquity becomes deeper yet, when we return to other scenes of the holy record, in which the powers of good and of evil are shewn in direct conflict with each other. The Son of God is manifested on earth, with a twofold purpose in relation to two different orders of beings,— "that He might destroy the works of the devil, and make us the sons of God, and heirs of eternal life[g]."

[c] Rev. xii. 9.   [d] St. John viii. 44.   [e] St. Jude, 6.
[f] 2 St. Peter ii. 4.   [g] Collect for the Sixth Sunday after the Epiphany.

During His ministry on earth, we see Him brought into contact with evil in two very different forms, as it exists in sinful man, and as it exists in the unclean spirits whose permitted visitations, as recorded in the Gospels, bring so vividly before us the true nature of that conflict, which He came among us to wage. Towards sinful humanity, He who was without sin Himself is ever drawn by the bonds of love and compassion. He is the friend of publicans and sinners; He comes not to call the righteous, but sinners to repentance; He tells us of the joy that is in heaven over one sinner that repenteth; He comforts the paralytic with the assurance "Thy sins are forgiven thee," and receives the weeping penitent with the words "Her sins, which are many, are forgiven; for she loved much." Behold Him, on the other hand, in the presence of that mysterious and terrible twofold existence, wherein the human form and the human organs of speech do but hide the presence and utter the words of the evil spirit possessing them. Mark the frightful shriek[h] and the words of horror and hatred, "What have we to do with Thee, Thou Jesus of Nazareth? art Thou come to destroy us[i]?" telling of the repugnance and recoil of the spirit of evil in the presence of the Holy One of God, and the stern answering rebuke, "Hold thy peace, and come out of him"—note the brief but fearfully expressive language of that graphic picture of another Evangelist, "*And when he saw Him*, straightway the spirit tare him; and he fell on the ground, and wallowed foaming[j]." Observe the demoniac of Gadara, seemingly under the influence of a double consciousness[k], as the suffering man, and as the instrument of the evil spirit possessing him,

---

[h] ἔα. See Bp. Ellicott in "Aids to Faith," p. 437.   [i] St. Luke iv. 34.
[j] St. Mark ix. 20.   [k] See Abp. Trench, "Notes on the Miracles," p. 171.

how first, "when he saw Jesus afar off, he ran and worshipped Him;" and then, as the words of power were uttered, "Come out of the man, thou unclean spirit," changing suddenly from the gesture of submission to the language of fear and abhorrence, "What have I to do with Thee, Jesus, Thou Son of the most high God? I adjure Thee by God that Thou torment me not¹;" and then observe the same man, when the devils had gone out of him, sitting at the feet of Jesus, clothed and in his right mind, and beseeching that he might be with Him;—do not all these pictures tell a fearful tale of that evil which existed before the first Adam fell, and for which the second Adam brought no redemption ᵐ? Do they not warn us how little we really know of the nature and origin of that sin which is in us and among us, with which we have walked hand in hand, till familiarity has half divested it of its horrors? May they not serve to assure or to rebuke us, if ever we feel disposed to doubt or cavil at the means which God has appointed for our redemption, by suggesting a deeper significance than lies on the surface, a significance in relation to the whole spiritual creation, evil as well as good, in those words of the Apostle concerning the Incarnation of the Son of God, "Verily, He took not on Him the nature of angels; but He took on Him the seed of Abraham ⁿ?"

How little we know, how little probably could be made known to our human apprehensions, of the real nature and spiritual sources of that conflict between good and evil, whose first earthly manifestation is revealed to us in the history of Adam's fall, may perhaps be faintly indicated, if we turn for a moment to that great poem in which human genius of the highest order

---

¹ St. Mark v. 6—8. ᵐ See "The Restoration of Belief," p. 358.
ⁿ Heb. ii. 16.

has striven to fill up the blank which divine revelation had left in the record of man's first disobedience. The tempter, who in the book of Genesis is simply described as the serpent who was more subtle than any beast of the field which the Lord God had made, appears in the poem of Milton with all the vivid personality of the apostate angel. His rebellion and fall from heaven; his bold defiance of God; his secret thoughts and declared purposes; his counsels to seduce the newly created race of man; his intrusion into Paradise; the details of his previous wiles and final temptation, are all minutely described with the combined power of poetic genius and religious zeal. Yet the effect of the picture, after all, is not that of the vice "which to be hated, needs but to be seen;" the author of evil, plotting, acting, suffering, never entirely forfeits the interest—we might almost say the sympathy—of the reader. And why? Because we feel that the materials with which the blank is filled up are, after all, borrowed from human nature and human impulses—depraved indeed, exaggerated, gigantic in their proportions, but still human. His pride, his envy, his revenge, his obstinacy, his despair, are but our own passions and our own vices on a magnified scale; our abhorrence of them is only that which would be called forth by great abilities, coupled with great wickedness, in one of our fellow-men. Contrast with this the portrait drawn, in a far less religious spirit, by a great poet of another country °,—the portrait of the mocking fiend, ever dogging the steps of his victim with the ready temptation, yet with no share in the feelings which give temptation its power,—that calm, passionless, subtle, scoffing intellect, with a sneer for all, and a sympathy for none—in the presence of such

° Goethe.

a being, we shrink and shudder instinctively, as though brought face to face with one of a different order from ourselves: we are just able faintly to apprehend the possibility that in a purely spiritual nature, apart from the appetites and desires and passions of humanity, there may be more of unmixed evil, more of the wholly devilish, than in all the pride of a Satan, and all the cruelty of a Moloch, and all the lust of a Belial, and all the covetousness of a Mammon.

But if this be so, what lesson does it teach us? Is it to find in the passions of fallen man an excuse for the sins to which they lead; to look lightly on our own evil nature, because it is not wholly evil; to confound the boundaries of virtue and vice, because the same human feelings may be subservient to the one or the other? God forbid! Is it not rather the lesson taught by the words of the Apostle, "Know ye not, that to whom ye yield yourselves servants to obey, his servants ye are to whom ye obey; whether of sin unto death, or of obedience unto righteousness[p]?" The conflict in which the first man fell, the conflict in which all his posterity are involved, is not merely a conflict between different principles in ourselves; it is not merely a struggle of our own lusts and appetites against our own reason and conscience; it is not merely a question of *self*-control or *self*-indulgence; it is the continuation of a conflict which began before Adam was, which had its source in a spiritual mystery before the human body was framed, or human passions had their birth,—a conflict, not between good and evil principles, but between good and evil beings, one or other of whom we must serve and obey in time and in eternity. Our human nature, in shrinking back from this thought of unmixed

[p] Rom. vi. 16.

unembodied spiritual evil, does but obey an impulse which God has implanted in it for good—does but testify that, whatever we may know, or whatever we may tolerate, of evil in this world in its human form, there is a depth and a mystery of evil, aye, and of misery, behind the veil of human thoughts and actions, which we cannot know now, but which we may know hereafter; that our human excuses and extenuations are but the disguises which serve to give an unreal appearance to that malignity which, unveiled, no human eye could bear to look upon.

Alienated as man is from God by sin, he is yet more alienated from the devil by humanity, that humanity of which He partakes who has no concord with Belial. As the servant of Christ, he obeys One who shares his nature, who has partaken of his feelings, his sufferings, his sorrows, his temptations; who "learned obedience by the things which He suffered, and, being made perfect, became the Author of eternal salvation unto all them that obey Him[q]." As the servant of Satan, he becomes enslaved to one of an alien and a hostile kind; a being whose nature we cannot conceive while the human consciousness still moulds our thoughts and furnishes our type of personality; whose malignity we cannot fathom while the human passion is still working within us, to disguise sin under the allurements of pleasure, to fix our thoughts on the sensual enjoyment, and to avert them from the spiritual evil; but which hereafter, when enjoyment, even · sinful enjoyment, exists no more, when passion can no longer rush to the objects of its gratification, when remorse cannot be drowned for a moment in the oblivion of passing pleasure, may be manifested in its true features to the clear perception of

[q] Heb. v. 8, 9.

evil affinity, like to like, the devil to the children of the devil.

The same conviction of the mysterious and inscrutable nature of evil, which is forced upon us when we would follow the poet in his attempt to soar on the wings of fancy to the supernatural world, is forced upon us no less, when we turn to the speculations of the philosopher, reasoning from what he knows, and within the limits of what he knows, concerning the triumph of sin in the natural world. "How it comes to pass that creatures made upright fall," says Bishop Butler, "... seems distinctly conceivablé from the very nature of particular affections or propensions. For suppose creatures intended for such a particular state of life, for which such propensions were necessary: suppose them endued with such propensions, together with moral understanding, as well including a practical sense of virtue, as a speculative perception of it; and that all these several principles, both natural and moral, forming an inward constitution of mind, were in the most exact proportion possible, i.e. in a proportion the most exactly adapted to their intended state of life; such creatures would be made upright or finitely perfect. Now particular propensions, from their very nature, must be felt, the objects of them being present; though they cannot be gratified at all, or not with the allowance of the moral principle. But if they can be gratified without its allowance, or by contradicting it, then they must be conceived to have some tendency, in how low a degree soever, yet some tendency, to induce persons to such forbidden gratification.... And thus it is plainly conceivable that creatures without blemish, as they came out of the hands of God, may be in danger of going wrong'." There is truth and wis-

[r] Analogy, pt. i. ch. v.

dom in this passage, as applied to human things from a human point of view. The needs of man's life, the constitution of man's mind, the working of man's motives and affections and appetites, are so analysed as to offer a reasonable explanation of the fall of a being such as man, even from a state of primitive innocence ; but it is the fall of man alone, or of beings like man, that is thus explicable : where the likeness to human nature ceases, the explanation ceases to be applicable. Our thoughts may be sometimes tempted to dwell on the history of the transgression of our first parents from this human point of view exclusively. We picture to ourselves the apparent lightness of the one positive precept which they were bidden to keep, the apparent weakness of the temptation by which they were induced to transgress. Simple indeed, and plain, and unadorned, and unaided by one word of philosophic theory or explanation, is that unpretending narrative of facts in which is recounted the temptation under which the first Adam fell—as simple, as plain, as unpretending, as that other narrative of that other temptation over which the second Adam triumphed. Yet both alike have one feature in common : the simple tale may be enhanced to what height the imagination may reach, by the thought of the presence of that subtle malignant spirit, bringing every power of evil to bear secretly and invisibly in aid of those suggestions and proffers whose outward expression alone we see. But go back in thought beyond the temptation and ·fall of Adam, to that earlier fall in which there was no temptation—what imagination can depict the conditions of the first transgression of a pure Spirit by the unsolicited resolve of his own will ? Surely in the existence of this spiritual wickedness in high places, there is a mystery of lawlessness which no effort of human thought is able to explain, or even to conceive —something not to be accounted for by that freedom of the will which is but the condition of the possibility, not the cause of the reality, of sin; not to be accounted for by those passions and propensions through which in man the flesh lusteth contrary to the spirit; something wherein the palliations and excuses with which men seek to gloss over human sin have no place; something which is not merely a wavering service, a lukewarm love, a will thwarted in the performance, a heart seduced from the allegiance which still it acknowledges; but a settled, implacable malignity, a constant unchanging resolve of defiance, a calm, steady, purposed hatred of good, of which all that human imagination can conceive of evil and misery is but as the flickering passing shadow to the fixed abiding substance.

Yet, God be thanked, over against this mystery of evil is that other surpassing mystery of godliness, "God manifest in the flesh." There is not merely enmity between God and Satan, between the spirit of good and the spirit of evil, but human nature also is permitted to take part in that contest—yea, is taken up into God, to be the means of carrying on His warfare and accomplishing His victory. "I will put enmity between thee and the woman, and between thy seed and her seed: it shall bruise thy head, and thou shalt bruise his heel." On one side of this prediction, the ever-brightening morn of advancing prophecy, the broad daylight of fulfilment, have in turn shed their rays; we know how much more is meant in these words than their first import conveyed to their first hearers; how "God sending His own Son in the likeness of sinful flesh, and for sin, condemned sin in the flesh*." But is

---

* Rom. viii. 3.

there not an unknown depth of significance on the other side also? And may not the mystery of that which we do not know, serve to guide our thoughts aright with regard to that which in part we know? Are we disposed to doubt or cavil at the mystery of our redemption? Are we tempted to ask why it should be necessary that He by whom all things were made should assume the nature of His creature, and die for the sins of men? Let us first ask ourselves to declare, if we can, what is the origin and nature of that sin for which He died; what is the character of that conflict which it needed such a sacrifice to complete. Beyond the mystery of sin in the flesh, lies the mystery of sin in the spirit. Above the evil from which we are redeemed, frowns the black shadow of that for which there is no redemption. The sin of man is atoned for, because man is not wholly evil; because that which taints and corrupts his nature is in it, but not of it; because humanity itself is not sin, nay, rather, is that through which Christ could destroy sin. But could we strip off this veil of humanity, and stand face to face with sin in its pure unmixed spiritual malignity; could we behold naked and open the real nature of that evil which has become the very form and essence of the Evil One's being,—that evil which, as thus existing, even infinite power cannot restore, even infinite love cannot pardon; could we see the spiritual antecedents and conditions of that great conflict which to our mortal eyes begins with man's fall and terminates with his redemption; could we estimate the value of our salvation by the full knowledge of that from which we are saved, well may we believe that, in the presence of that fearful sight, the voice of doubt would be hushed for ever, the anxious questioning would no longer shape itself to consciousness; one only thought could have place, one only voice could find an utterance. On this side, the Redeemer, Perfect God and Perfect Man ; on that, the arch-enemy, perfect evil. On one side, the triumphant hymn, "Worthy is the Lamb that was slain ;" on the other, the despairing cry of those who "shall seek death and shall not find it ; and shall desire to die, and death shall flee from them." Pray we then, believing in the reality of this conflict of good and evil, looking forward surely to the final consummation—pray we while it is time, in this our season of penitence, to Him who was wounded for our offences and smitten for our wickedness, that He "will deliver us from the curse of the law, and from the extreme malediction· which shall light upon them that shall be set upon the left hand ; and that He will set us on His right hand, and give us the gracious benediction of His Father, commanding us to take possession of His glorious kingdom : unto which may He vouchsafe to bring us all, for His infinite mercy. Amen."

SERMON III.

The Kingdom of Darkness Prevailing.

JOB i. 7.

"And the Lord said unto Satan, Whence comest thou? Then Satan answered the Lord, and said, From going to and fro in the earth, and from walking up and down in it."

IT is important to note the exact point in the sequence of these Lent Sermons at which to-night we have arrived. You have had your thoughts drawn to the personality and active malignity of our spiritual adversaries; you have seen those spiritual adversaries manifesting themselves out of their thick darkness in the first encounter with Adam and Eve, and obtaining a victory over the man and the woman whom the Lord had made.

Upon the success of the tempter in Paradise followed the erection of a kingdom. Of that kingdom we are to speak to-night. It is a kingdom, under whose baleful shadow the race of men sank lower and lower from the mount of light, into an ever-deepening abyss of impurity and superstition,—a kingdom lasting in unbroken force from the sin of Adam, until the coming of Christ.

We may fitly go for a text to the Book of Job. That book occupies a very remarkable position in the Bible with reference to this subject. It is the one Book whose scenery and action lie outside the visible Church of God. There is in it no mention of the covenant people, no reference to any institutions of revealed religion. The Book was doubtless written for the edification of the Jewish Church, but the edification was to consist in the exhibition of the utter inability of good men by their own wisdom to find out God, and to justify His ways to His creatures. All the dialogues between Job and his friends are successive pictures of human reason struggling vainly to unravel the perplexities of a world which is but the wreck of what God made it. The whole Book is a voice as it were from without the ark, crying to those within of the darkness that may be felt, which, independent of revelation, encircles every dispensation.

And so the sublime vision with which the Book opens, is to be viewed not only as the substructure of the after afflictions of the Patriarch Job. Far deeper is its significance. It is the laying bare of the secret power to which all the perplexities, all the ignorance, all the sin of the great old world of heathenism owed their origin. "There was a day when the sons of God came to present themselves before the Lord, and Satan came also among them. And the Lord said unto Satan, Whence comest thou? Then Satan answered the Lord."—The reply of the fallen archangel is eloquent of the profoundest of all mysteries, the mystery which philosophy ever stumbles at, but without which it vainly attempts to solve the hundred riddles of human life; the mystery of a power in the world which is not God's power; of a presence among mankind which is not the presence of man or of God; of the dwelling amongst us of another being of a real and true personality, who is not sin, but the author of sin, of whom all that we call abstract evil, is but the creation and the shadow. "Whence comest thou? And Satan answered the Lord, and said, From going to and fro in the earth, and from walking up and down in it."

Here, then, we are face to face with the subject of to-night. Satan walking abroad upon the earth; it is the Scripture account of the kingdom of darkness prevailing.

Now our object this evening must be to enquire into the constituent elements of this kingdom. The Bible appears to intimate two such elements; let us consider each.

I. The first element, then, of the kingdom of darkness prevailing between Adam and Christ, would seem to be the gradual withdrawal of the manifested presence of God.

Amongst the few verses in which the Holy Ghost has communicated to us all that we are permitted to know of the state of man in Paradise, there is nothing which more seizes upon the imagination than the record, "And they heard the voice of the Lord God walking in the garden in the cool of the day," —"the sound of the Majestic Presence approaching nearer and nearer[a]." All that the words mean we may perhaps never fathom; but thus much they certainly teach, a sensible manifestation of God's presence, not then new to our first parents. Adam heard God before he saw God. He knew God's voice, i.e. recognised the sound of the manifested Presence, from having been familiar with it before.

Again, after the Fall and the expulsion from the garden of Eden, there are still traces of the same manifested Presence. It was the source of Cain's despair, "From Thy Presence shall I be hid." The burden of his sentence was that he must go far away from the

[a] Patrick.

spot where the Shechinah of the divine majesty yet appeared, and to which, by the ordinance of sacrifice, the creature, until excommunicated like Cain, was still privileged to draw near.

And there is reason to believe that this sensible manifestation of God lasted until the Deluge. So perhaps is to be understood the decree, "My Spirit shall not always strive with man," (or rather, shall not always abide among men,) "seeing that he also is flesh;" as though, in consequence of the determined sin of the creature, his utter abandonment to the lusts of the flesh, there should be thenceforward a further deprivation of the abiding Spirit. It is moreover to be noted that amid all the desperate wickedness of the antediluvian world, there is no mention of idolatry; whilst immediately after the Deluge we find it commencing. Perhaps the tower of Babel itself is rightly conceived by some expositors [b] to have been designed as a temple, the substitute of a material point of unity and worship in place of the lost Presence.

This then seems to be the Scriptural account of the first period of man's sojourn upon the earth. The world before the Flood!—dimly through the mist of years it rises up, a world in which the strength of man and the vitality of man were amazingly developed, for the life of seven or eight hundred years was but one feature of a life far exceeding our own in all physical powers. It was a world, too, which preserved still a relic of the lost Paradise in a visible Presence of the Holy One, yea it may be an intercourse (hence the trespass of the sons of God with the daughters of men) such as we vainly strive to realize with the angels of heaven. But it was a world whose increasing corruption drove that

[b] Patrick.

Presence finally away from this lower creation, in mingled judgment and mercy; so that when the cleansed earth emerged from the baptism of waters, and the race of Adam started upon the second stage of their probation, it was with diminished powers, and a shortened tenure of existence, and the face of the Lord God hidden from them. And hence, first, we may trace the deep darkness which fell upon the nations. Hence, too, we may see the force of the words in which it is said at the beginning of his wanderings, "The Lord appeared unto Abraham." That was the earliest manifestation of the Presence since its withdrawal from the antediluvian world; the beginning of the re-establishment of true religion upon the earth. And so you find that in the chosen family, where alone the worship of the one God was preserved, where alone the profound darkness was broken, there was from time to time, to the patriarchs in their travels, to Moses in the wilderness, upon the mercy-seat in the tabernacle, a manifestation of the Divine Majesty vouchsafed; while the voice of the heathen world, in its vague speculations, in its disquietude and unrest, was still that of those who seek vainly for a something lost: "I go forward but He is not there, and backward but I cannot perceive Him. On the left hand where He doth work, but I cannot behold Him. He hideth Himself on the right hand, but I cannot see Him."

We may not answer the question wherefore, if this withdrawal of the manifested Presence was the beginning of the kingdom of darkness, God still age after age held back the face of His throne. It may be that in the mystery of the Divine nature lie hidden necessities for these veilings of the Lord God from a fallen creation; that even as now by the Church is made known to the principalities and powers in heavenly places the manifold wisdom of God, so in that hiding of the Lord God during long ages from the great mass of the race of the apostate, lessons may have been learnt, lessons about sin and holiness, which were a guard and a warning to angels and archangels on their thrones of light. It may be that these hidings of God were essential even for man, to make him value aright, and be thankful enough for the great epiphany of Deity in the face of Jesus Christ. The utter incapacity of man to create for himself God out of his own inner consciousness was never more demonstrated than when it was seen that left to himself man invariably conceived of God in ways the most sensual and degrading, not clothing the divinity of his own imagination in whatever might seem most reverend and august, but shaping Him (as St. Paul says) like to birds and beasts and creeping things. The hiding of God— it was the perpetuating for long ages the kingdom of darkness, but it was the laying deep for ever and for ever the foundations of the kingdom of light.

II. The second element of the kingdom of darkness is an increasing development of Satanic influence. As the face of God was withdrawn, the infernal presence waxed more and more oppressive. It is necessary here to observe how unmistakeably and how uniformly the New Testament speaks of the heathen world not as merely practising evil, but as lying under the dominion of evil spirits, and of the Incarnation of Christ as the undermining and shattering that dominion. Thus our Lord Himself, upon the return of the Seventy with the report of their success, at once points out the true nature of their victory: "I beheld Satan as lightning fall from heaven[e]." That first mission had struck at

[e] St. Luke x. 18.

the heart of his power. So again, just before His own Passion, He announces while yet the voice from heaven thrilled on the ear of the startled multitude, "Now is the judgment of this world; now shall the prince of this world be cast out[d]." So, a little later, He speaks of His sufferings as an encounter with the great adversary: "The prince of this world cometh, and hath nothing in Me[e]." The title "PRINCE OF THIS WORLD" points to a dominion once, it may be, lawfully exercised by Satan as God's vicegerent over this planet, and still attempted to be asserted in spite of his apostasy. And the same idea is taken up by St. Paul, "It is the God of this world who blinds the minds of those who refuse to believe[f];" "It is the prince of the power of the air who worketh in the children of disobedience[g]." They are the rulers of the darkness of this world with whom the Christian conflict is waged. And there is another class of texts, not to be passed by, which speak of physical suffering as the result of Satan's usurped mastery of the earth. The woman with the spirit of infirmity is the woman whom Satan hath bound. The ability to tread upon serpents and scorpions is the grant of a capacity to tread upon all the power of the enemy. And in the Epistle to the Hebrews we have the devil spoken of as holding even the power of death.

Now the question is not whether this or that passage may be got rid of, as expressed in compliance with the notions of the day, but whether these passages all together (and they might be multiplied) do not point uniformly to one truth as taught by Christ and the Apostles, of a veritable supremacy obtained by evil spirits over mankind, a kingdom of darkness set up by them

[d] St. John xii. 31. [e] Ibid. xiv. 30. [f] 2 Cor. iv. 4.
[g] Ephes. ii. 2; vi. 12.

not growing out of man's corrupt nature alone, which the Cross of Christ was to shake and finally cast down.

And when we proceed with the clue which Scripture thus gives, to thread the labyrinths of that old world, it is remarkable how all holds together, how this theory of a kingdom set up by Satan and his angels is the key which unlocks a thousand dark places in the records of humanity. We are to recollect that when the posterity of Noah started forth from their first settlements to people the void earth, they carried everywhere with them their belief in the *Unseen*. From the plains of Shinar they went out, the fathers of mankind, through the silence of primeval forests, into solitudes where the human voice had never sounded. There was no manifested Presence of the Holy One in their new resting-places to give life and light, but the tradition of that Presence had not died out, and the deep instincts of the human soul responded to the tradition. So that never, we may believe, did man sink to the level of the beasts, having no belief in, no fear of, the Invisible and the Eternal. And upon this profound conviction of the human soul, the great adversary forthwith began to work. He could not obliterate the innate consciousness of God's existence, but he could distort the true instinct, and draw men to the worship of false gods. Man could not live without God. He must by the very constitution of his being have gods to go before him; but he might be satisfied with a lie. Hence the rise of idolatry. For what was idolatry in its deepest, truest sense? It was Satan thrusting himself into the place of God, and diverting to himself the homage of the creature. "The fall of angels," says Hooker, "was pride. And these wicked spirits the heathen honoured instead of gods, some in oracles, some in idols, some as household gods;

in a word, no foul and wicked spirit which was not in one way or other honoured of men as god, till such time as light appeared in the world and dissolved the works of darkness [h]." This is the essence of the sin of idolatry. It is not as Scripture views it, as the early Church, which was confronted with it, considered it, the faulty worship through unworthy similitudes of the true God, but the bowing down of the worshipper to rebel spirits whom God had cast out. Accordingly, every vicious lust was not so much personified in some idol. This is a shallow way of regarding the fact. The truer conception is, that one seducing spirit and another procured themselves to be served each according to his own nature, until bolder and bolder waxed the prince of the kingdom, and in the confessed worship of the naked evil principle the triumph of the great rebel angel was complete.

To this same Satanic agency likewise are we in all probability to refer that strange mixture of truth and deceit which are found in the ancient oracles, the practice of magic and witchcraft, against which not as mere imposture God thought it not unworthy to speak to Moses His sternest laws of prohibition. It is not necessary, on the one hand, to endorse the vulgar notions of the manner in which the agency of Satan was herein exhibited; neither, on the other hand, if we believe (and Scripture is plain as to this) that there are undefinable ways of communication between the human soul and the spirits of evil,—that surely as the Holy One can breathe into us His promptings, no less can the Enemy whisper unto us his temptations; if we believe this, then there is no difficulty in tracing to the same dark agency that entire system of mingled truth and fraud, and lying wonders, by which as in an inextricable web the souls of men

[h] Hooker, bk. i. ch. 4.

were for centuries held captive, so as to be unable to shake off the terrible bondage, even when the light of heaven broke into their prison-house.

And hence too it appears, why the religion of the old world was ever accompanied with viciousness of morals. This is the great fact of heathenism—its temples, its sacrifices, its priesthood, did nothing to raise the standard of moral goodness. Call to mind for a moment the utter disregard of human life. I speak not of the licence of war. The horrors of the amphitheatre, the slave slain for the fish-pond, are the fairer index of an utter forgetfulness of the origin, nature, and destiny of man. Look, again, at the entire disruption of domestic ties; the lusts (of which it is a shame to speak) not merely indulged in by the bad, but countenanced by philosophers and teachers; the pollution which the streets of buried cities, exhumed from the sepulchre of ages, testify unto us, not as shrinking from observation, but as boasted before the sun. Look, yet again, at the stains which defile the noblest literature which human genius has created. Is it only the infirmity of our nature which these things demonstrate, and not rather, as Scripture intimates, the presence of fouler spirits wresting to their will the noblest spirits among men.

And observe, lastly, how the difficult subject of diabolical possession squares with this. It cannot, I believe, be ascertained at what precise period we first find mention of the possessed with devils. The Book of Tobit contains an early instance. But if it be true that the power of Satan increased step by step, idolatry becoming more gross and the worship of evil more confessed, it is in harmony with this that his power over the bodies of men should likewise augment, until at the close, when the night was far spent and the dawn at hand, it manifested itself in fiercer visible convulsions of flesh and spirit, and so, when the Stronger than the strong came down, ministered unwittingly to Him an additional means of demonstrating His supremacy.

Here, then, are some of the features of the kingdom of darkness as it prevailed from the fall of the first Adam to the birth of the second. On the one hand, we have the Presence of the Lord, retiring as it were from His dishonoured temple; and on the other hand, the fallen archangel offering himself to the creature's instinct of worship, and gradually drawing to himself and to his host the homage of the nations, making worship the instrument of vice, until the adoration of the evil principle in its nakedness, and the corporal possession of men's bodies, marks the culmination of the power of the kingdom. Oh, as I contemplate that old world in its greatness and its littleness, its reachings forth after truth, its prostration to evil, its occasional perceptions of a holier, purer life, its incapacity to live it, what does it resemble so much as some grand intelligence no longer master of itself, but while yet retaining a dim consciousness of its own terrible malady, under the fierce impulse of madness going greedily after every deed of violence and of shame. "And the Lord said unto Satan, Whence comest thou?" And the answer is the answer which revelation and reason alike re-echo. "Satan answered the Lord, and said, From going to and fro in the earth, and from walking up and down in it."

Two great lessons flow from what has been said. First we may learn the vanity of all attempts to get rid of the mysteries of religion. The foundations of our most holy faith lie deep in the profoundest secrets of eternity. They touch upon truths wholly outside this world of time; the ineffable relationships of the Only Begotten Son to the Almighty Father; His first manifestation to the heavenly hierarchy; Satan's refusal to worship; the fall of a third part of the angelic host; the consequent hostility of the apostate spirit to the new creature man, issuing in a temporary triumph. And you do not grasp the whole truth unless you take into view all these more hidden verities. To pass them by in a vain attempt to conciliate modern rationalism is only to isolate the central truth of the Incarnation from those other cognate truths which give it its due proportion in the chain of divine providences. We cannot estimate aright the work of Christ unless we connect it as Scripture does with other agencies. We cannot sympathize with His triumphs, unless we realize the true character of His foe. The mystery of godliness stands in a strange correlation to the mystery of iniquity. The divine personality and mission of the Son, can scarcely be viewed apart from the personality and reign of Satan. You weaken rather than strengthen the cause of Christianity, by trying to sever between it and these darker things of God.

The second lesson is this—the utter incapacity of anything short of the faith of Christ, and the grace of Christ, to cleanse and lift up man's life. It is sometimes asked, "What has the Gospel done?" Why, the Gospel alone has purified society, as (thank God) in spite of our unworthiness, it has been purified. Civilization could not do it; philosophy tried, and failed; aye, and confessed its failure. "No one," said Seneca, "is of himself sufficiently strong to emerge from the slough. Some other must stretch forth a hand; some other must draw him out[1]." What is this but crea-

[1] Sen., Ep. 52.

tion groaning for its deliverance, the wisest of this world crying out for a wisdom loftier than itself? It failed, that old civilization, with all its intellectual resources. It had no motive, no hope, no faith adequate to the task, above all, no superhuman power working in it to do for man what he could not do for himself; so even when it saw the road, it could not walk in it; when it enunciated rules of virtue, it could not practise them. "It is one thing," (says St. Augustine, contrasting the Church and the world,) "from a wooded steep to see one's country of peace, and not to find the path into it; and another thing to pursue the road which leads there under the guardian care of a heavenly master."

And if this be true of the entire race, so (oh, believe ye it!) is it true of each separate man. What all its intellect could not accomplish for that old world, its exaltation and its cleansing, neither can science or refinement or intellectual pre-eminence do for the individual soul. "The ancient learning," again says St. Augustine, "had no tears of confession to tell of, no broken spirit, no contrite heart, no sanctifying Spirit, no Cross of redemption[k]." And by these things alone does man live; by these alone can the individual soul be rescued, as the world was rescued, from the dominion of darkness, and made fit for the inheritance of the saints in light.

[k] Confessions, lib. vii. 21.

SERMON IV.

The Coming in of the Son of Man.—His Conflict and Victory.

ST. JOHN xii. 31.

"*Now shall the prince of this world be cast out.*"

IF a person of ordinary intelligence and of candid mind had the Gospel narratives for the first time brought to his notice, he would observe one central character, round whom the rest are grouped, moving onward through a variety of incidents with the simplicity and reality of historical fact. Wonders, so to speak, play around Him; but miracle is not His ordinary element, nor the material out of which His biography is constructed. Plain truth, calmness and solemnity, compassion and charity, these are His characteristics. From time to time, He gives, in His converse, indications of familiarity with things other than those with which human experience deals. His heavenly Father who has sent Him, the holy angels of God, the hostile powers of evil, with these He seems acquainted as we are not acquainted. He speaks with authoritative knowledge of God's will and God's acts. He declares absolutely what is done round God's throne in heaven. He deals with the unseen world not as the inheritor, but as the corrector, of common belief. And all this, as we say, *de suo*. No one revealed aught to Him, of no one has He learnt anything; "Verily I say unto you" is

His preface, when He has to speak of things unknown to man.

Now I imagine our observer would at once see that there is no possibility of divaricating the sayings and testimonies of this Speaker, so that we may accept some of them and reject others. Either all is matter of fact, or else all is romance. If He has this authoritative knowledge of His heavenly Father who sent Him, then it would be unfair to suppose that when He couples together His Father and the holy angels, He is in the same breath speaking of the living God and of the creations of a fictitious mythology; it would be as unfair to suppose that when He in moments of equal solemnity speaks of spiritual foes, of the devil and his angels, He is dealing with unrealities. It would be plain to our observer, as I hope also it is plain to us, that he who should assert this might—indeed must, if he follow his system up to completeness—maintain that the Father who sent Him, indeed that every thing and person of which He spoke, except those which were palpable to human sense, were the creatures of His own imagination, and have for us no reality.

I make these prefatory remarks, to shew you how entirely impossible I believe it for one who is a Christian in any sense to regard our Lord's conflict with the powers of darkness otherwise than as an objective reality; and that I may shew that our simple Christian faith on this matter is a wiser and more consistent and more rational thing, than the current half-belief of the day.

And now, entering on our main subject, let us first notice where we take it up. Darkness covers the earth, and gross darkness the nations. The powers of evil seem to the eye of sense to have prevailed. God's fair creation has been desolated by them. The moral state of the heathen world is too fearful to contemplate. The intellectual energies have either been perverted to subserve that moral degradation, or where they have been striving for good, have been baffled, and have sunk down in despair. The people of the living God, who possess His covenant and His ordinances, have indeed had the demon of idolatry cast out of them by the sharp discipline of the captivity, but have become the prey of the more malignant demons of hypocrisy and worldliness, and their last state is worse than their first. Nor was this unhappy age without more positive inroads from the unseen powers of darkness. The facts of demoniacal possession, as brought before us in the Gospels, are distinct and undeniable, on the supposition of any basis of truth at all underlying the personal history in those narratives. They are accurately distinguished from mere disease of a cognate form; the phænomena of casting out evil spirits in no particulars resemble those of miraculous healing. We have in the wretched victims all the symptoms of an oppressed, and in some cases of a redoubled consciousness; and the usurper of their personality quits them reluctantly, and even in some cases not without the infliction of agonized cruel suffering.

Such was the age; the Augustan age of man's pride, and pomp, and power, and skill; the darkest age and climax of misery of all that man was made for as an immortal being. Spiritually, we seem to have arrived at a period in the history of creation resembling that when the earth was without form and void, and darkness was upon the face of the deep.

But upon the darkness there arose a great light, shining in it, but not comprehended by it; hated by the darkness, persecuted by the darkness, eventually extinguished by the darkness, but springing up again in renewed splendour, and passed on from hand to hand by the children of light, and yet to be passed on, even till all be light and no dark place remaining.

It is to trace this conflict of light with darkness in the person of Him who is the light of the world, that we are to address ourselves this evening. May He Himself shine among us and within us, while we are so employed.

Without accepting the view held by some of the ancient fathers, that the great adversary was kept in ignorance of the nativity of our Lord, we may at all events take it as meaning for us thus much—that except in the one particular of the malignant agency of Herod, no details have reached us of the conflict between Him and the powers of darkness during His infancy and youth. For us that conflict begins at the decisive and mysterious period of His temptation in the wilderness. And observe how entirely that temptation, in the form in which it is related to us, bears out all that we know and believe respecting Him. In Him was no sin, not any even the least motion towards sin. It was quite impossible then that He, when He was tempted, should be "drawn away of His own lust and enticed." That temptation was not and could not be any struggle between the better and the worse mind within Himself. Whatever analogy in point of time it may have borne with those seasons of choice and decision which usher in the young man's active life, in this respect it had none; it was no deliberation between the worse and the better path, no hesitation between enjoyment and self-denial, no wavering between present ambition and the fulfilment of the prescribed course. Throughout the whole, the tempter came to Him in person, came to Him from without. Evil did not arise within Him, but was presented to Him, presented through the outward senses, which in Him, as in ourselves, were avenues open for the impression of ideas on the mind within. And in that we read that He suffered, being tempted, we must conceive of that suffering not as an inward conflict with inclination to evil, not as a warring of the law of sin within the members against the law of God, but as the deep anguish and loathing of the holy soul at the contact and intrusion of evil, as the grief and revulsion of the pure spotless life and heart at the withering poison of selfish and unhallowed suggestions made to Him by the foe. In Him was an absolute barrier, beyond which the turbid waves of evil could not pass; but against it they chafed and raged, disquieting and troubling His spirit, and driving the human will within the shelter of the divine purpose.

It has perhaps not enough been noticed, that in our Lord's conquest over the foe at His temptation, there is the hiding rather than the putting forth of His power. The temptations come upon Him with all the accessions of the unusual and the wonderful; the forty days' fast, the giddy pinnacle of danger, the mountain vision of pomp; but His weapons are far other in character. He steps not out of the rank in God's army which the humblest Jew might have occupied; His defensive weapons are the words of the law under which He was born into the world, "It is written," "It is written again;" and to the final presumptuous attempt of the enemy to turn His life into treason, and His obedience into rebellion, He opposes that one central command, by loyalty to which the three in Babylon had foiled Nebuchadnezzar, and the seven and their mother had resisted Antiochus, "Thou shalt worship the Lord thy God, and Him only shalt thou serve." And hereby is the Lord's conflict with Satan in the wilderness distinguished from others that follow, that His resistance was purely human; that all the display of power was on the side of the foe; that what He did is no more than we may do when tempted to sin; no more than the holy youth did when he said, "How can I do this great wickedness, and sin against God?" And hence it is that in this battle and victory has rightly been seen Paradise regained; that it has been felt that, although much was yet to be done before the powers of darkness were finally bruised under foot, yet here, where the Lord as man vanquished man's ancient enemy, was the true counterpart of Eden, where our first father was tempted and fell.

. The narrative of the temptation in St. Luke ends with a notice of especial importance in this view of the subject —that when the devil had ended all the temptations, he departed from Him for a season. The explanation of this has been usually, and I believe rightly, found in the words which our Lord used to those who came to take Him in the garden, words be it remembered also found in St. Luke's Gospel—"Now is your hour, and the power of darkness."

In passing to our Lord's public ministry, and there tracing the conflict, we are at once struck with the new phase into which it seems to have entered. Now the wicked spirits know Him as the Holy One of God, come forth out of the possessed at His bidding, are subject to His appointed heralds, the twelve and the seventy, commanding them in His name. We have His Divine power here prominently displayed: "Thou dumb and deaf spirit, ἐγὼ ἐπιτέλλω σοι, it is I who say unto thee, come out of him, and enter no more into him ;" and, we read, the "unclean spirits when they saw Him, fell down before Him, and cried saying, Thou art the Son of God. And He straitly charged them that they should not make Him known." So that during the public exercise of His ministry, His divine glory and power seem to have overawed and overborne the hosts of evil. But we are hardly therefore justified in supposing that His own soul, and His private hours were free from the harassing of the subtle foe. He Himself gives a name to the traitor Judas, which seems to point to the fact that the enemy was from the first contriving, by means of that wicked instrument, the betrayal of Jesus to death. And in St. John's Gospel, the several stages of the dark treachery are distinctly ascribed, first to Satan having put it into his heart, at a certain time, and then, as it proceeded, to Satan entering into him, i.e. fully possessing him for evil. Again, from certain other expressions of our Lord we gather the continued watchfulness and subtlety of the malignant foe. When St. Peter, having but newly received praise for his confession of Jesus as the Son of God, ignorantly and over-boldly ventured to rebuke the Lord for the expressed anticipation of His sufferings, the very same words by which the tempter was formerly defeated are again uttered, and a significant reason added : "Get thee behind Me, Satan ; thou art an offence unto Me, for thou savourest not the things that be of God, but the things that be of men." The carnal selfish view which would shrink from suffering—this is again presented in all its loathsomeness before our Lord's sight, and He recoils back from it again with horror. Under the same head we may also number two other of His sayings. When He was charged with casting out devils by a league with the prince of the devils, He laid down clearly and carefully that ineffaceable distinction which there was between His work and Satan's work, His kingdom and Satan's kingdom. It is impossible that light can be partly darkness, or darkness partly light. Satan, in the possession of men's souls and the glory of this world, is represented as the strong man armed, keeping his goods in peace; the Lord is the stronger than he, taking from him his armour wherein he trusted, and spoiling his goods. The other saying is the argument, not altogether dissimilar, by which, in the Gospel of St. John, He turns upon His enemies the charge that He had a devil, and turns their malignity against Himself to their father the devil, who was a murderer from the beginning. By these, and by sayings and incidents like these, we may see how close the conflict always lay to our Redeemer's soul, even during that time when it was not personally and prominently renewed; how it appeared in the contradiction of sinners against Him, in the treachery of His friends, in the conspiracies of His enemies. We know nothing indeed of the secrets of His inner life; but we may presume to say that when He continued whole nights in prayer to God, the inward conflict was not unfelt by Him, but rather that He was waging it from time to time in deep places far removed from human sight, and that on each occasion faith and resolve gained the victory over human infirmity, new dangers were braved, and new difficulties encountered.

One, and certainly the chief of such wrestlings of spirit, has been recorded for our instruction; one, respecting which Jesus Himself said, "the prince of this world cometh, and hath nothing in Me;" one, too, bearing a certain analogy with the former scene of temptation. The weakness and the exhausted frame, crushed down with the horror of the bitter cup of suffering, now close at His lips, prompted at the first moment the prayer that it might depart from Him. Three times does the temptation come on Him. After each He seeks for sympathy in the affection of His disciples. All the while the human will is waning, the holy resolve is waxing onwards. The human will was not sin, was not inclining to sin; but while the spirit was willing, the flesh was weak, was open to the tempter, was keenly watched by the malignity of the foe. At this point the real victory was gained. Never were words sublimer in their simplicity than these of St. John, "Jesus therefore knowing all things that should come upon Him, went forth unto them."

And now we come to that with respect to which the saying in our text was uttered, "Now shall the prince of this world be cast out," which was the adversary's triumph, and yet the Lord's glorification; the culminating point of the foe's enmity, and the greatest victory of the Saviour's love. The Cross of Calvary is the centre of the world's history; to it all before converges; from it all that follows shall radiate. There the Saviour triumphed openly over the powers of evil. "Through death He vanquished him that had the power of death, that is, the devil;" through the blood of His Cross He abolished the ancient enmity between God and man, brought in by the evil one; and by His divine power He came up out of death with that nature of ours which He had taken upon Him triumphant over death; and with it upon Him He ascended up where He was before, carrying that nature of ours into the presence, and upon the very throne of God. And now all things are subject to Him, in heaven and in earth, and under the earth, i.e. in the realms of darkness and the lost ; and all this lapse of the ages, and all these changes of empires, and all this progress of man, are but the steps whereby all things are being put under His feet, that He may reign with His saints in that kingdom which is the one promise of the world, and for which all creation groans.

And meantime, my brethren, how stands the conflict? where is now the foe? what are we to think of him and of ourselves? The Cross of Christ hath passed ; the Son of Man is at the right hand of God. The foe is not as he was. His power is broken—broken as respects man in general, broken especially as respects the Church and people of Christ. From the day when the Lord was taken up from us even till this day, has the kingdom of evil been crumbling away before the grace of Christ's Gospel. Slowly indeed, and, as far as we ought to be fellow-workers with that grace, unworthily of Him who hath founded it, does this blessed progress go on towards the final triumph ; still are the dark corners of the earth full of cruelty, still in vast unevangelized tracts does the strong man armed seem to be keeping his goods in peace ; but age after age abundant grace is given in answer to the devout prayers and missionary efforts of the Church, and the dark spaces are narrowing before advancing light. Where the Church in her fulness has been set up, in Christendom itself, we witness more advanced stages of the great conflict, and the kingdom of light in further development. Age by age the maxims and practices of selfishness and cruelty are giving way, and the leaven is gradually spreading through the lump of human society. And in the advance of the great Christian body, the individual Christian doubtless also gains advantage for his share of the great conflict. But the laws of spiritual being are not altered. Man has not ceased to be, under redemption, what he was in himself and his personal attributes before redemption. We are still responsible, open to solicitation from evil, open to influence for good. The soul of man is drawn upward by God's grace, is drawn downward to ruin by God's enemy. About ourselves, as once about our Lord, are the hosts of darkness leagued together against every one of us; not yet is the abyss sealed, or the foe chained down. Each one, by himself and for himself, must maintain the conflict with the spiritual enemy. It is the first law of our moral being, that by temptation, by suffering, and resolve, by power exerted, and rebutting the enemy, each one of us is to rise to good and to God; each one of us is to win his way to the everlasting reward. Where then is the difference? What is it to us that the Son of Man was brought in? What to us is His conflict and victory? In our inner hearts, when we are assailed by divers temptations, of what import to us is that portion of the world's history in which He lived and died, any more than any other portion? What is He to us, any more than any other great and pure person who has fought the good fight and won the glittering crown? Let our answer to this be clear and definite, or it is no answer for us: or it will not speak peace to our hearts in the hour of our trial.

What He is to us in that hour, what we feel Him to be to us in every hour of failing strength, of agonized prayer, of wrestling and yearning with God, He is, not because He has set us an example, not because we wonder at Him, not because we love Him merely, but because on Him in that conflict, on Him in that victory, on Him as He bled on the cross, on Him as He burst the tomb, on Him as He rose through the cloud that received Him, on Him as He now sits on the throne of

God, He bears our human nature entire, summed up in Him; so that His conflict is our conflict, His victory our victory, His acceptance before God's throne our acceptance, so that we are more than conquerors through Him that loved us. And thus, when I am harassed by the foe, when temptation oppresses and weak nature is giving way, there is One to look to, there is One to lean upon, there is One to commune with, there is One to get strength from, who is mine; mine for all I can need in all the depths of my nature, because He is in, and lives through, all that nature in His Deity; God with me: mine, not because I have won Him, but because He has won me and bought me, and paid His blood for me, by an everlasting covenant, firm as the covenant of the earth and the sea; so that out of weakness I can stretch out my hand and His hand shall grasp it, and out of faintness I can utter my feeble cry, and He shall answer; and for all my wants there comes supply, and for all my sins there comes pardon, and in all my troubles there comes peace, and in all my struggles there comes victory, out of His fulness, for in Him all fulness dwells.

You will hear, my brethren, from those who shall come after me in this Lent season, how He has provided for this conflict to be carried on during these ages of waiting in the body of which He is the Head. You shall hear how the promise of the Father, won by Him, came down on His people, the oil of His anointing descending to the skirts of His raiment; and you shall hear who were set up to dispense and to carry on that grace, and what are the aids and the weapons of the conflict, and what the crisis and final event.

Meantime, and that seems especially the matter to be pressed upon us to-night, whatever be the means and appliances appointed for our warfare, and none of them may be safely neglected by us, let us in them all, let us through them all, be ever, each one for himself, looking to Him the Captain, who is gone up before us—the Son of God, the righteous Head of our common nature. This, my brethren, is for each one of us the one thing above all others needful, that we should know Him for ourselves. We may hear of Him by the hearing of the ear; we may be sound in the faith respecting Him; we may love His ordinances, and rejoice to meet round His holy Table; but in all these, and above all things, it is Himself that we must seek and find; Himself that we must know and commune with, and walk about with in our common life. In temptation here, in trial and conflict anywhere and at any time, there is but one sure safeguard, binding together the affections, knitting up the resolves with everlasting strength, and that safeguard is the abiding consciousness in the soul, of that glorified Human Form on the right hand of God, the living lustre of His eye, the sight of His hand pointing our way, the blessed sound of His voice cheering and commanding us: "To him that overcometh will I give to sit down with Me on My throne, even as I also overcame and am set down with My Father on His throne." With this assurance, the weakest among us may become strong, and the feeble one may vanquish a thousand. "If God be for us, who can be against us?"

SERMON V.

The Kingdom of Light set up.—The Conflict and Victory of its Faithful Children.

ST. LUKE xxiv. 49.

"Behold, I send the promise of My Father upon you: but tarry ye in the city of Jerusalem, until ye be endued with power from on high."

MAN'S power had been weighed in the balance, and had been found wanting. Minds, as acute, as rich, as varied in their gifts, as any which God had created, had done whatever could be done in the way of intellect. The intrinsic beauty of goodness, its fittingness, the moral duty of seeking it for its own sake, and as the end of man, had been taught with all the power of Greek intelligence. The schools of philosophy had decayed. Their lessons had become mostly powerless on those who taught in them[a]. Socrates, Plato, Aristotle, were to use a world-wide influence within their own province, the human intellect. Their instantaneous failure, and three centuries of decay, had shewn that they were not to be the moral teachers, or the regenerators of mankind.

Rome had tried what man could do on the moral side. The stern, unloving warriors, strict with them-

---

[a] "230." Plutarch. Comparat. Thesei c. Rom. c. 7. "520." Val. Max. Hist. v. 6. 1. "521." A. Gell. Noct. Att. xvii. 21.

selves as with others, had stamped on their polity and their people a rigid morality. It is a marvel to us, how at least fidelity on the wife's side could become to such an extent a heathen virtue. Contrast with the miseries and iniquities revealed and fostered by the English Divorce Court, Roman faithfulness, through which, in a hot climate, divorce was unknown for two hundred and thirty, some say, for five hundred and twenty years. But the hard, icy virtues of the republic, frost-bound by the necessity of discipline, had, under the warm glow of prosperity, melted into one stream of universal dissoluteness. The failure of a mighty effort leaves the greater hopelessness. It is a calm historian, who turned away sickened from his own times, (about our Lord's birth,) in which, by a rapid but complete declension, "we can bear," he says, "neither our vices nor remedies[b]." Another, who could speak freely of iniquity at which he afterwards connived, says, "Will the wise ever cease to be angry, if once he begins? All is full of guilt and vice; more is committed than can be constrained. A great war of wickedness is waged; daily the lust for sin is greater, the shame less. Casting out all regard for aught good or just, lust fastens where it will. Guilt is no longer stealthy; it parades itself. Iniquity is so sent abroad, has such might in the hearts of all, that innocence is not rare only; it is *not*[c]." A wide-spread nature-worship, whose centre was the mystery of reproduced life, consecrated sensuality; the philosophy of Stoics or Epicureans, the most rigid or the most lax, alike justified degrading sin[d]; human nature cast itself

[b] Liv. Præf. ad Hist. v. fin.

[c] Seneca de Ira, ii. 8. It is thought to have been one of his earliest works.

[d] See Döllinger Heidenthum und Judenthum, b. v. c. ii. p. 328.

willingly into the black pool, to whose edge its gods beckoned it on.

Even Jewish life had decayed. Its most esteemed sect was rigid in externals, in love heartless, in inward life reprobate. Ambition and hatred of their masters had desecrated the prophetic promises of spiritual victories into temporal hopes. An Epicurean sensuality had bound down the hopes of a third class to the things of this life.

It seems as though God had waited until there could be no hope of the moral regeneration of man from man, to work His own marvellous work. As He employed the poor, the illiterate, "unlearned and ignorant men," "the foolish things of the world, and the weak things of the world, and base things of the world, and things despised, yea, things" accounted as if they "were not"—to confound the wise and the mighty, and that which held that it alone *was*, in order "that no flesh should glory in His Presence," so He allowed man's keenest intelligence, and strongest moral power, the instruments which He had Himself formed in the natural order of things, to try their utmost and fail, that the Divinity of Jesus and His revelation might stand out the more clearly, after the recognition of the impotence of what was grand, powerful, beautiful, perfect in its way, but —human.

What was lacking, was not so much understanding, or motives, as power. The unwritten law, written in men's consciences (however, here or there, it was obscured even in its primal laws), was clear. "I see what is better, and approve it; I follow what is worse," is a confession of human nature, just as our Lord was coming. Dissoluteness had not yet quite eaten out among the people the old beliefs in a sort of heaven and hell, the Elysian fields and Tartarus; but it was the powerless echo of a mighty truth, whose dying sounds moved neither heart nor intellect.

Not, then, the inherent might of truth was wanting to the soul; man had already more truth than he availed himself of. Not persuasive motives; what man had already, were powerless. Motives will not enable one paralyzed to move. The Gospel *has* constraining motives, stronger than hope and fear, love for Him who so loved us. Yet love, too, has its constraining power to those alive, not to one dead. And human nature was dead to good, in its trespasses and sins.

What then was needed, besides all revealed truth, was "power." Our blessed Lord came to give us that power, being Himself "the wisdom of God, and the power of God [e]." He came to give a new beginning to our nature, by Himself taking it. He took our human weakness, to impart to it His Divine might. The power which He was and had, He, by His manhood, lodged in it. Mankind was redeemed by weakness; it was converted by power. The power had been hidden in His humiliation, for the suffering of His atoning Death. The reason for shrouding it was removed on His resurrection. Then He who "was of the seed of David according to the flesh," was, "according to the Spirit of holiness," i.e. according to His holy and Divine Nature, "defined" or marked out to be "the Son of God *in power* by the resurrection of the dead [f]." This power He laid as the groundwork of the apostles' mission; "All power is given to Me in heaven and in earth. Go ye therefore, and disciple all nations; I am with you alway, unto the end of the world [g]." This power, which was His, He bade His Apostles wait until they

[e] 1 Cor. i. 24.   [f] Rom. i. 3.   [g] St. Matt. xxviii. 18—20.

should be invested with it. "I send the promise of My Father upon you; but tarry ye in the city of Jerusalem, until ye be endowed with power from on high [h]." And this power was the indwelling of the Holy Ghost. In Him they were to be baptized, immersed, flooded. "Ye shall be baptized with the Holy Ghost not many days hence [i]." "Ye shall receive power, after that the Holy Ghost is come upon you [j]."

Doubtless this power included the gifts of superhuman works wrought by the Apostles, as St. Peter speaks of our Lord Himself: "Ye know, how God anointed Jesus of Nazareth with the Holy Ghost and *with power:* Who went about doing good, and healing all that were oppressed with the devil; for God was with Him [k]."

Its first expression was in the gift of tongues; but the gift of tongues was only the vehicle of the Divine power. "We do hear them speak in our own tongues *the wonderful works* of God." St. Paul, in speaking of what "Christ" had "wrought by" him "to the obedience of the Gentiles, by word or deed," distinguishes these two; "in the power of signs and wonders," "in the power of the Holy Spirit [l];" an outward and supernatural power of miracles, and an inward transforming power of the Spirit.

But the outward miracles were the body, not the soul. They were God's glorious works of Divine love attesting His Presence; the rending of the rocks, the earthquake, the fire, were but the forerunners of the Lord; He was not *in* them; God manifested Himself in the still small voice [m]. The mighty works in the Gospel accredited God's messengers, as come from Him; they disposed men's hearts to listen; but the might

[h] St. Luke xxiv. 49.   [i] Acts i. 5.   [j] Ibid. 8.   [k] Ibid. x. 38.
[l] Rom. xv. 18.   [m] 1 Kings xix. 11, 12.

which converted the heart, was the Gospel itself, spoken in the words of God to hearts which He opened to receive it. The Gospel itself was "the power of God unto salvation[n]." "The preaching of the cross was to them who perish foolishness; but to us who are saved it is the power of God[o]." "My word and my preaching were not in persuasive words of man's wisdom, but in demonstration of the Spirit and of power." It was not "persuasion," but "demonstration;" not demonstration of human reasoning, but a divine power and energy of heavenly grace[p]. It was an Almighty and ever-present power, working in and through them. "I became a minister of the Gospel," says St. Paul, "according to the gift of the grace of God, which was given to me, according to the inworking of His power[q]." And this power they bore about with them in this our decaying frame, "in earthen vessels, that the transcendingness of the power," they say, "may be of God, and not from us[r]."

Yet they were but great eminent instruments of Divine power. "The Spirit of the Lord spake by" them, "and His word was on" their "tongue[s]." Speaking with Divine power, they brought over the world to God; savages they persuaded to learn wisdom; all the whole order of the world they altered. But they were only triumphant captains in the war of the Lord, under the great Captain of our salvation, chiefs of the Church, lights of the world. They who so bare Christ upon their

---

[n] Rom. i. 16.   [o] 1 Cor. i. 18.
[p] "The Divine word (1 Cor. ii. 4) saith, that what is spoken (although in itself true and most persuasive) is not self-sufficing to reach the human soul, unless some power from God be also given to the speaker, and grace engerminate in what is spoken; this too being, not without God, infused in those who speak profitably."—(*Orig. c. Cels.* vi. 2.)
[q] Eph. iii. 7.   [r] 2 Cor. iv. 7.   [s] 2 Sam. xxiii. 2.

tongues, who had that seraphic love, doubtless have their thrones with cherubim and seraphim. But the "power" itself they speak of, as the common possession of the Church. For it was one and the same Spirit which, having been given without measure to our Lord, was thenceforth to be poured forth fully upon His Church, giving to the whole Church (when acting as a whole) that inerrancy which He gave to His Apostles, streaming, in its sanctifying powers, upon all its members; in all, supernatural, lifting up the soul above nature, uniting it to God, and restoring His likeness in it. In the Apostles, above all, were those gifts of the Spirit, which were for the benefit of others. Yet these, too, all but infallibility, continued on in individuals too in the Church since; nay, even in its lesser members; for if any one speaks so as to reach a brother's soul, our Lord's words still come true of him; "It is not you that speak, but the Spirit of My Father who speaketh in you."

But in the conflict which belongs to all, the Apostles needed the same armoury as we; we are gifted with that same endowment whereby they trampled upon Satan, subdued the flesh, despised the world. To them, too, weakness was Divine might. It is one of the few personal revelations to himself which St. Paul records, "My grace sufficeth for thee, for My power is perfected in weakness [t]." "Therefore," he subjoins, "most sweetly will I rather boast in my infirmities, that the power of Christ may reside upon me." Apostles had the same weaknesses as we, save those which any of us entail on ourselves by evil habits; we have, for victory, for eternal life, for glory, for that which is the glory and the joy of eternal life,—the love of God, the same helps as

[t] 2 Cor. xii. 9.

they. "The least grace," it is a dogmatic saying [u], "is able to resist any concupiscence, and to gain eternal life."

But St. Paul, who glories in his own weakness, exults in the superabundant might of grace deposited in the Church for each of us by virtue of its union, and ours in it, with Christ, its Head. Inspiration itself (since it must needs use our human words) does not seem to suffice him, as he piles up words upon words to utter as he may, that which is unutterable—the transcendentness of the might of the grace of God to usward. It is not to be uttered in words. As

> "He who loveth, knoweth well
> What Jesus 'tis to love,"

so he who has used grace, knows something of the power of grace. Its fullest power *that* saint alone can know, who here below used it most, and whom it has uplifted nearest to the throne of God. The Ephesians knew it. They were a source of unceasing thanksgiving to St. Paul for "the faith in the Lord Jesus, which was among them, and the love to all the saints [v]." And therefore he prayed for them, that God would reveal to them by an inward illumining of the eyes of the heart, —what? Some fresh truth? Some larger knowledge of Himself? No : but what is the transcendent greatness of the power of His grace which they knew already. "That the God of our Lord Jesus Christ, the Father of glory, would give you the spirit of wisdom and revelation in the full knowledge [x] of Him ; having the eyes of your heart enlightened, so that you may know, what is the hope of His calling, and what the riches of the glory of His inheritance in the saints"—(this relates to

---

[u] S. Thom. 3 p. q. 62, art. 6, fin. comp. q. 70, art. 4, conc.   [v] Eph. i. 15, 16.   [x] ἐπιγνώσει, v. 17.

what eye hath not seen nor ear heard, the glory of those already perfected, but he adds, as equally an object of revelation, the might of grace which God puts forth here below)—"and what the transcending greatness of His power to usward the believing, according to the working of the strength of His might, which He worked in Christ, in that He raised Him from the dead, and placed Him on His Right Hand in the heavenly places, far above all principality and *power* and dominion, and every name which is named, not only in this world but in that which is to come, and hath subjected all things under His feet." And *Him*, Who is thus above all might, He has given to be the Source of the might lodged in all of us who from that time to the end are "the believers." "And Him He gave to be Head over all to the Church, which is His body, the fullness of Him who filleth all things in all."

He parallels "working" with "working;" the greatness of His power to usward who believe, with the might of His power whereby He raised Christ from the dead. The might of grace operating in us was involved in the might which gave life to the dead Body of Jesus. "According to," he says; as the effect is in the cause. And what might? The might of Him Who is above all might which can be named or conceived. And why should this might, shewed forth in our Lord, redound to us? Because we belong to Him. He is our Head, we are His members; and He vouchsafes to account something to be lacking to Himself, until the last redeemed sinner, the price of His Precious Blood, shall be gathered unto Him, because the Church, i.e. the whole multitude of His redeemed, is, as being the body of Him Who is our Head, the fullness, or filling up, of Him, Who, in His Godhead, filleth all things in all.

We have seen the height, look now at the breadth of this power, how he prays for those of another Church [y], who had the same faith in Jesus, the same love towards all saints, in whom the Gospel had been not only fruit-bearing but growing since they first heard of it. He prayed unceasingly, that the grace and the knowledge of the will of God should spread through their whole spiritual being, and *that*, with power. "That ye should be filled with the thorough knowledge of His will in *all* wisdom and spiritual understanding, to walk worthily of the Lord to *all* pleasing, fruit-bearing and increasing in *all* good work, empowered in *all* power according to the might of His glory, to *all* endurance and long-suffering with joy [z]." The glory of the might of Christ is manifested in being put forth to strengthen us; the power, wherewith we are empowered, is in conformity with the might of Christ, and universal.

And this he prays even for his most recent converts [a], that "our God would count them worthy of His calling, and fulfil all good pleasure in goodness, and all work of faith in power." And this power, lodged in us, stands opposed to our mute shrinking from exertion. " God did not give us a spirit of cowardice, but of power, and love, and of correction [b]."

This power they had, having been once powerless. The Epistles embody spiritual facts. They appeal to people's souls, what they had been, what God had done for them, what they had become. They had been, for the most part, like others. Heathens, they had lived in heathen sins. They had been dead to all spiritual things, in trespasses and sins [c]; sold under sin [d]; slaves

---

[y] Col. i. 4, 6. [z] Ib. 9—11. [a] 2 Thess. i. 11. [b] 2 Tim. i. 7.
[c] Eph. ii. 1, 5; Col. ii. 13. [d] Rom. vii. 14.

of sin[e]; sin ruled over them by a law to which they were captive[f].

They *all*, St. Paul says emphatically, "we all," i. e. all alike, Jews and Gentiles, "were occupied in the lusts of our flesh, doing the wills of the flesh and of our minds, and we were, by nature, children of wrath, like the rest[g]." Nay, they had not only their inherent powerlessness. As they had now the powerful inworking of God the Holy Ghost for good, so aforetime they had the inworking of an evil spirit for evil. As the patriarchs walked to and fro with God, so now people "walked according to the course of this world, according to the ruler of the power of the air, the spirit, who now worketh[h]," not in them who had been freed from him but, "in the children of disobedience."

And so St. Paul bids them be tender to the heathen, as having once been what these still were, "shewing all meekness towards all men; for we too were formerly without understanding, disobedient, erring, slaves to divers lusts and passions, passing our whole lives in malice and envy, hateful and hating one another[i]."

Men were amazed, St. Peter attests, at the change, as they are now too at the conversion of one, Christian in name only; and, as they do now also, they calumniated them. "Sufficient is the past time, to have worked out the will of the heathen, by walking, as ye did, in lasciviousnesses, lusts, drunkennesses, revellings, carousals; wherein they are amazed, that you rush not with them into the same slough of profligacy, speaking evil of you[k]."

But from all this Christians had been set free, and free they remained. Their two conditions, their past

[e] Rom. vi. 17, 20.   [f] Ib. vii. 23, 25.   [g] Eph. ii. 3.   [h] Ib. 2.
[i] Tit. iii. 3.   [k] 1 Pet. iv. 3, 4.

and their present, were as different as darkness and light, death and life, utter slavery and perfect freedom, prostrate weakness and superhuman strength, degradation below man and elevation above man. And between those two states there had been an act. Were there no history besides the Epistles, these would be records of the marvellous transformation of countless multitudes at one and the same time. They had been what we should shrink to think of; they became what we should long to be. And one act had passed between. Holy Scripture says not only, "Ye *were* ungodly, ye *are* now godly; ye *were* profane, ye *are* now devout; ye *were* sensual, ye *are* now spiritual." It says that their past and their present were severed by a great act, in which *they* had only been recipients, with their own free-will accepting the free gift of God.

"God shone in our hearts," they say, "called us, wrought and moulded us for this very thing, Who also is He who gave us the earnest of the Spirit[1]; He loved us and made us acceptable to Himself in the Beloved; co-quickened us in Christ, anointed us, sealed us." "The law of the Spirit of Christ freed me from the law of sin and death." On the other hand, they say of themselves: ' we *were* compassionated, *were* made free from sins and from the law, and *were* made servants to righteousness; we *were* reconciled, *were* justified, *were* washed, *were* sanctified, *were* saved; we received the atonement, an anointing, the spirit of adoption, access to His grace; their old man had been crucified with Christ, co-interred; with Him they had been co-interred, with Him co-raised; in Him they had been re-created unto good works; with Him they had been clothed; in Him made rich; in Him they had been all baptized into one body,

[1] 2 Cor. v. 5.

all had been made to drink into One Spirit; by His Spirit they had been sealed to the day of redemption [m].' And what was their condition now? You know the deep expression of intimate love and union—they were "*in Christ.*" To Him they were united by His Spirit dwelling in them, because they had been made members of Christ, closely united to Him as members to their Head, of His flesh and of His bones, because, as He says, "Whoso eateth My Flesh, and drinketh My Blood, dwelleth in Me, and I in him... He that eateth Me, shall live by Me [n]."

Of all this, the poor world could, of course, know nothing, as neither can the natural man now. But it saw the change, and then it scorned, reproached, ridiculed (as it does now), counted Christians as madmen, or—it was converted. While some were moved by miracles or the fulfilment of prophecy [o], and others, "yea, oftentimes were drawn by an over-mastering power of the Spirit against their will changing their ruling mind suddenly from hatred of the Word to willingness to die for it [p]," others were moved by the superhuman life or superhuman change, which they saw. "Why mention the countless multitude of those who changed from profligacy, and who learned continence? For Christ called not the righteous, nor the sober to repentance; but the ungodly, and profligate, and unrighteous. But that we should be endurant of evil and subservient to all, He saith on this wise, 'To him who smiteth thee on the one cheek, turn to him the other also.' Nor doth

---

[m] See the fuller development of the bearing of these statements in Holy Scripture, in Pusey's "Scriptural Doctrine of Holy Baptism," pp. 155—175, § "Passages which speak of Christian gifts, as having been bestowed in the past."

[n] St. John vi. 56, 7.   [o] St. Aug. in Ps. cxlix. 13.   [p] Orig. c. Cels. i. 46.

He will that we should be imitators of the bad, but He bade us through patience and meekness to lead all from shame and lust of evil things; which, moreover, we can shew in the case of many who have come among us, who changed from violent and oppressive men, having been conquered, either when they traced the endurance of their neighbour's life, or the strange patience of fellow-travellers when defrauded, or when they made trial of those with whom they were engaged in business [q]."

Celsus mocked at the Gospel for receiving sinners; "Perfectly to change nature," he said truly, "is all-difficult [r]." Truly, for man it is impossible. But, then, on that very ground, the change, when it did exist, was Divine. "When we see those words which he saith are uninstructed, (as if they were charms,) to be filled with power, impelling whole multitudes at once from profligacy to a life wholly well-ordered, from injustice to goodness, from a recreant unmanliness to a mind striving to despise even death for the sake of the godliness revealed among them, how can we fail to admire the power lodged therein? For the word of those who first ministered and toiled to found the Churches of God; yea, their preaching was with persuasiveness, not such as is the persuasiveness of those who proclaim the wisdom of Plato or any other philosopher who had nothing but human nature. But the demonstration in the Apostles of Jesus, having been given by God, was persuasive from the Spirit and power. Wherefore their word, or rather the Word of God, ran most swiftly and most forcibly, changing through them many of those to whom sin was nature and custom; whom man could not have changed even by punishing,

[q] St. Justin, Apol. i. 15, 16.   [r] In Orig. iii. 69.

but the Word transmade, forming and fashioning them after its own will [s]."

Even persecution was the harvest-seed of the Church, not by enlisting sympathies, (which were none, in a people brutalized the more by the exhibition of Christian suffering, except when an executioner here and there came in nearer contact with a sufferer,) but because the superhuman fortitude drew people's thoughts. "Every man who beholdeth so much endurance," is an appeal to a Roman governor, cognizant of facts, "being struck with some misgiving, is kindled with the desire of enquiring, what is the cause of this? and so soon as he discovereth the truth, himself also immediately followeth it [t]."

That change which passed over each converted soul, so that it hated what it before craved; had serene mastery over the passions, to which it was before enslaved; loved to be without what was before the miserable solace of its misery; loved what it before had no taste for;—this was a spiritual fact which could be known only by experience. The experience of the senses tells us the things of sense; the experience of the soul tells us the things which pass in the soul. Beforehand they seem impossible; experienced they are known. "I," says St. Cyprian, of his heathen state [u], "when I yet lay in darkness and blind night, and tottering and uncertain with erring steps reeled on the sea of this tossing world, ignorant of my life, alien from truth and light; according to my then ways, I thought what the Divine mercy promised for my salvation, altogether difficult and hard, that one could be new-born, that, quickened to a new

[s] In Orig. iii. 68.   [t] Tertull. ad Scap. end, p. 150, Oxf. Tr.; comp. his Apol. end; and others quoted there, p. 105, note a, Oxf. Tr.
[u] Ad Donat., § 2, 3, pp. 2, 3, Oxf. Tr.

life by the laver of healing water, one should lay aside what he had been before, and, while the frame of the body still remained, should be changed himself in heart and mind. How is so great a conversion possible, that suddenly and rapidly *that* should be put off which, either being part of our natural selves, has hardened in the neglected soil, or, if acquired, has long been engrained, inveterate through age? These things hold secure by deep, far-penetrating roots. While allurements still cling tenaciously, love of wine must needs invite, pride inflate, anger inflame, rapacity disquiet, cruelty stimulate, ambition delight, lust cast headlong. These things said I ofttimes with myself; for, being held entangled with very many errors of my former life, whereof I did not believe that I could be freed, I humoured the vices which clung to me, and, in despair of aught better, nurtured my own evils, as being now my own offspring, born in my house."

The method of his conversion St. Cyprian does not relate. For he relates only his own evils, and the re-creating good of God. But see the contrast of powerlessness and power. "But after that, the stain of the former life having been wiped away by the aid of the life-giving water, a light from above, serene and pure, poured itself into my forgiven breast, after that the second birth re-formed me into a new man, drinking in the Spirit from heaven, then forthwith, in a marvellous manner, things doubtful assumed steadfastness, things closed lay open, things dark shone with light; what seemed aforetime difficulties offered facilities; what was thought impossible seemed now achieveable, as it *was* to own, that *that* which, being born after the flesh, lived subject to guilt, was of earth, *that* which the Holy Ghost was now quickening had begun to be of God. Thou knowest and ownest with me, what that death of crimes, that life of virtues, took from me, what it gave me. Now, by the gift of God, not to sin has begun to be the work of faith, as, before, to sin belonged to human error. Of God, of God, is all my power. From Him I live, from Him I have strength, from Him, in that vigour which I have received and ingathered, I have, even while placed here below, some foretokens of what is to be hereafter."

Such are two pictures of powerlessness in his heathen state, of self-power as a Christian, which St. Cyprian gives of himself. Ask yourselves, my sons, "which of the twain belongs to me?" I do not mean to ask as to any of the coarser outbreaks of sin. Deadly sin is compatible with a decent exterior, deserving in some things to be thought well of, a general wish to save the soul, a hope that it will be saved, a wish to be on God's side somehow, a doing some things for God, a vague yearning after Him. And yet some one unmastered, ever-mastering sin, makes the heart not whole with God, defiles perhaps the temple of the Holy Ghost, the body; it wounds the conscience, cripples the soul, withdraws it from intercourse with God, its Life, chases away the Holy Spirit, scares from Communions, the great preservative against deadly sin, or makes the soul go to them faithlessly, hopelessly, unprofitably.

But whether it be some one sin, bodily or even spiritual, which holds you back, whether it be a general torpor, a predominance of sense, a personal ambition which dulls you as to things spiritual, or a general self-complacency which stunts your growth, if your religion is not one of power, it must be that you have not, generously and without reserve, admitted Christianity as a whole into your souls. For "the Gospel is the power of God unto salvation." Christ, of Whom men boast in name, is the Power of God; and "might" is one of the seven-fold gifts of the Spirit, and God clothes His own with the whole panoply of the Divine armoury. Contrariwise, it is to be part of the self-deceit of the last days, to own religion as something which *should* form the soul, "having or holding," St. Paul says, a "formativeness[x] of godliness, but having" practically denied or repudiated "its power." Perhaps it may be some eclecticism out of Christianity, some new-modelling of the old truths, giving new, unmeaning, alien meanings to the old doctrines. Perhaps it will think that it renders homage to our Lord, because it owns, while it criticises as a superior, some of the virtues of His Humanity, and will deem that it shews Him reverence in pronouncing " Ecce Homo[y]," while it has less of awe of Him than Pontius Pilate who crucified Him, and puts Him to more deliberate shame. But whatever that would-be "formativeness of godliness" may be, which the times of Antichrist may invent, be sure that a powerless religiosity is a sign of belonging not to Christ, but of being still under the power of the evil one. "His servants ye are, whom ye obey." There is a strong one who was bound and spoiled, and there is a Stronger than he, Who overcame him by His Death, and bound him. But bound though he be, while he has no power to hurt thee without thy will, he still masters those who place themselves within his grasp. Flee him, and he cannot follow thee. Betake thyself to Jesus, and the blasted one crouches at the presence of his Conqueror and his Judge. Mistrust thyself, but mistrust not God's Al-

---

[x] μόρφωσιν.   [y] My ground for thus warning the young as to the character of one single book, was, that even respectable journalists had been misled, and were misleading them. My words apply to the book only, not to the author, of whom and whose motives I know nothing.

mightiness. Look well whether there is any part of the Divine armoury which thou hast neglected? Hast thou mistrusted the omnipotence of prayer, or forgotten meditation on the love of God for thee, or thoughts on the four last things, which close and must close this fleeting life, Death, Judgment, Heaven, Hell; or on God's aweful holiness, trifling irreverently with His sacred attributes, and neglecting His inward calls; or forgetting Him from morning to evening, all the more confidently because thou rememberest Him a little then, and this thou thinkest must needs be enough, and God could not ask for more; or going to a monthly slovenly Sacrament, forgetting almost beforehand, but most certainly afterwards, Whose Presence was to be and was vouchsafed to thee; or holding on a little while by strength from God, and then, through unwatchfulness or tampering with evil imaginations, falling into the same sins as before? Or hast thou secretly thought that the real remedy for thy relapses would be, as others have done, to confess thy sins, and interpose thy Lord's absolving Voice, "Thy sins be forgiven thee," between the living and the dead, thy heap of dead putrefying sins and thy future of life, and hast held back for some shame or awkwardness, or secret pride?

It is a hard thing to say, (God grant that it may not be so!) but I more and more fear that what is wanted in so many, amid this powerless religiousness, is an entire conversion of heart. "Thou shalt love the Lord thy God with all thy heart, and with all thy mind, and with all thy soul, and with all thy strength; and thy neighbour as thyself." Where is this whole-hearted, loyal obedience, when self is stealthily enshrined in so many hearts, and God seems to be made for man, not man for God? A "weak Christian" were a contradiction in terms. For to be a Christian at all is to be a member of Christ, Who is Almighty God; it is to have a claim to *His* might, Who has all power in heaven and earth; it is to have Him for your indweller, Who is all-holiness, all-hallowing. To be a weak Christian is to have but a weak will to be a Christian, to have been made a Christian, yet half to repent of the love of God towards thee in making thee a Christian. Lean on Him, look to Him, watch unto Him, Whose strength is made perfect in weakness, and past weakness shall not hinder thee. He beholdeth thy conflict Who willeth to crown thee; He Who upheld the martyrs in their sufferings will uphold thee. Only be thou strong in the Lord and in the power of His might; He will overcome in thee Who bid thee "Be of good cheer; I have overcome the world." He saith to thee, "To him that overcometh will I grant to sit down with Me in My throne, even as I also overcame, and am set down with My Father in His throne."

Only be earnest now, at once, as if the yawning gulf of hell were open before thee, and thou couldest only cross it on that narrow wood, thy Saviour's Cross. He holds forth His nail-pierced Hands unto thee; He bids thee "come, and I will uphold thee." Only remember Him; and now, for His love's sake, remember those the wearied victims of their own weak will and of man's lusts, who long to be freed from their sickening existence, and who may yet be *His*, Who died for them and for us [z].

[z] There was to be a collection for a Penitentiary.

SERMON VI.

The Powers of Darkness Prevailing over the Disobedient.

ST. JOHN iii. 19.

"And this is the condemnation, that light is come into the world, and men loved darkness rather than light."

THIS language will at once be recognised as specially belonging to the beloved disciple, by whom in a peculiar manner our Lord Jesus Christ is set forth under the title of "the Light," "the true Light," "the Light of the world;" and His kingdom, as the kingdom of light. And in this respect he seems, as in so many other points, in his fervour, his tenderness, and deep prophetic insight, to have resembled and caught the spirit of Isaiah, who in passage after passage, kindled the gaze of Israel of old, to look towards the coming Light, as if he himself saw its orb still lingering below the distant hills.

And yet in this comparison of the Lord of Life with the material light of this world, there are involved both a contrast and a mystery.

When the sun is up, the whole hemisphere acknowledges its presence, and is irradiated by its beams. Darkness and night flee away. The birds go forth to meet the day with songs; the flowers expand themselves to drink in the light; the unreasoning creatures welcome the glad influence, for these have long learnt to obey the law of God. But with man, and in the moral and spiritual world, it is otherwise. Though the sky be radiant with the manifestation of the Lord of Life, and earth lit up with the beauty of salvation, yet many dark places remain unvisited; in many a soul the light does not enter, or if it enter, is again expelled; there is an active power of resistance which opposes itself, and claims a divided empire, and contests the heavenly influence, as though it were invading a territory within which it could claim no authority, and no allegiance.

Scripture, as we know, recognises throughout its record this power of moral resistance to the divine light; nay, more than this, it even seems to assert that when the light does not irradiate, it rouses the spirit of ill to intenser activity, and renders the darkness more deep. The evil spirits cried out, and vented their rage more fiercely at the presence of Jesus. Our Lord recognised the presence of the prince of darkness, as bearing rule for a season, when He told the Jews who came to arrest Him, "This is your hour, and the power of darkness." St. Paul told the Thessalonians of "the mystery of iniquity already working." The same apostle, seeing the effect of the gift of more abundant light, announces that "By the law is the knowledge of sin;" and that while to some the Gospel was "a savour of life unto life," to others it proved "a savour of death unto death;" just as, in the analogy of nature, the same warmth and moisture that endue with fresh vigour and fertility the living plant, only hasten corruption and decay in the dead and withered branch.

We see, then, the contrast between the material and spiritual light, as they severally shine on this dark world; we see, too, the mystery that is inherent in the permitted resistance to the latter. A mystery indeed it is, yet not peculiar to the Christian faith and the laws of Christ's kingdom, but inseparable from the condition of man as in a state of probation in this world, and involved in the fact of the very existence of evil; and therefore though it be insoluble by the reason, is not to be disputed, not to be cavilled at.

Rather let us recognise it; for in recognising it we learn our real condition and danger; and may find a safeguard even in contemplating the sad examples which exhibit the subtle power and deadly triumph of that evil which, as it wrought and prevailed in Paradise, still lurketh in the Church of Christ, and as a beast of prey, goeth about seeking whom it may destroy.

I. See then, shortly, how this power of darkness, ever since the Sun of righteousness hath appeared, has struggled to quench the light, and to retain its old dominion. We may notice it in the Church at large. When viewed on this side, its history presents but a dreary retrospect; and some too fondly looking for a reign of peace and glory as the token of any real reign of Christ, have been led to doubt whether the kingdom of God has indeed really come. But when our Lord declared, "For judgment am I come into the world," He pointed to those struggles and contests, those siftings of the spirit of evil, those strivings of the spirit of grace and life, which would mark the progress of His kingdom, and try and test the character and faith of every age, and of every soul. And so it has been that, age after age, Satan and his angels have tried to subvert the power and the truth of God; sometimes from without, and sometimes from within. At one time the light of truth has been assailed by a philosophic mysticism, seeking to corrupt the faith it could not gainsay or overthrow. At another, it has been overlaid by superstition, or almost extinguished by brute ignorance. Then has ensued a period of licentiousness and violence doing despite to the spirit of grace and purity; or one of cold indifference, when faith in the life-giving truths of the Gospel has been scorned as fanaticism; or again another, when a false light of reason and of science has claimed to itself to be the true and the sole light that lighteth every man. These have prevailed, and do prevail; and some souls have yielded to their seductive power, and surrendered their birthright.

But over the Church at large, and the faith once given, they have not prevailed, and will not prevail. These are indestructible; the gates of hell cannot prevail against them. And in such conflicts as these, we witness the unwearied assaults of those spirits of antichrist that are in the world, striving against the power of the Spirit of God,—trying, testing, and judging the Church, or special portions of it, or individual souls within it; proving the wheat and tares, and preparing all for that great day of judgment and of separation, when "righteousness shall be brought forth as the light, and judgment as the noon-day."

II. But now to bring the subject home to ourselves as individuals. This same conflict between darkness and light is going on in each; in each, sin is lurking and allying itself with the powers of evil without, and thus aiding them to draw us back to slavery and perdition; in some alas, how successfully, how fatally!

Let us note, then, this perilous and downward course; let us, for our warning, and to fill us with godly fear, mark the power of evil as it makes its assaults, and seeks to enslave the soul which Christ has purchased, and to which the Holy Spirit hath been given. And in order to give direction to our thoughts, let us trace it shortly in those three principal faculties of the soul of man, the *affections*, the *reason*, and the *will*.

1. And first in regard to the *affections*. It is here commonly that evil places its first footing, for here is the inner sanctuary of man's being, here the secret power that colours his thoughts, and excites the desire, and prompts the will. And here accordingly, especially in the ardent and imaginative, the forms of evil are ever ready to array themselves in their most seductive hues. The lust of pleasure, the lust of praise, the lust of ease, the lust of envy, the lust of unsanctified affections, these are some of the forms in which the spirit of evil seeks to seduce the heart and the affections from what is holy, and pure, and just, and of good report. And when any one of these has seized the imagination, and bribed the affections, what remains but that passion go foward to its end over the ruins of better resolutions. The soul, as of Demas, forsakes Christ, " having loved this present world ;" the things unseen are lost sight of in the glare of things seen; future hope is given up for present enjoyment ; the birthright is sold for a mess of pottage ; the grapes of Eshcol are despised for the cucumbers and melons of Egypt ; and the soul drifts away from the anchor within the veil, and its light and its love die away within, till he who once knew how to approach the High God, and looked to die the death of the righteous, fights and falls, like Balaam, in the ranks of the enemies of God.

To remind you that this downward course is one of increasing swiftness, that the sluice once opened, the waters swell till desolation spreads around, is but to repeat a truth so common as to lose all its force. But if you would make an effort to persevere at all, and not yield yourselves at once to the wiles of the tempter, beware of the first opening of temptation, watch the first shootings of the root of bitterness, guard the imagination from what is false, dreamy, self-indulgent, impure. Any one unresisted sin, whether it be of outward and positive transgression, or the indulgence of an unsanctified temper, the desire of ease, or favour, or pleasure, be it the active purpose that goes out after forbidden enjoyments, or the weak indulgence which yields to the seduction of the moment, and waxes slack in prayer or in public devotion, is a surrender to the enemy. How easy, alas, is this to us all! How often has prayer seemed to be thrown back upon us unanswered, and watchings to be fruitless, and better resolutions powerless, and hopes disappointed, till we have been tempted to lay down our arms in very weariness! Who of us have not seen instances of this falling away amongst their acquaintance, or felt it in a degree in themselves, till looking back on the faith and fervour of early youth, they feel that they are further off from God than they once were.

2. Then there is also the yielding and the enslavement of the *reason*. Let it be firmly impressed on our minds that reason is not naturally antagonistic to faith. In children it seems to be identified with faith, or, as far as it is exercised, to impart to it only strength and support. In them, the unwarped instinct testifies of God. Nature to them is (as has been said) "the living garment of Deity." With David, they hear His voice in the storm, and own His footsteps in the wind, and His tabernacle in the "pavilioned plains" of the sky. This harmony of the two it is of the last importance to maintain. It may be that subsequent investigation may tell the more instructed mind that God is not so

near in these phenomena as faith once deemed; that certain physical laws intervene; still that He is behind and above them all, that these are but manifestations of His will, and tokens of His presence, this, for our soul's health let us ever hold fast. And it is one great aim of the power of evil, the arch-deceiver, to separate what should be one; to divorce reason from faith, and to declare its independence.

It is no part of ours to deny or speak lightly of that great gift of reason, one of the guiding lights of the soul, which God hath imparted. But if it be dissociated from other gifts and other instincts, faith, consciousness, imagination, intuition, it becomes at once a tyrant and a slave. "While it promises liberty, itself is the servant of corruption[a]." It is then tied down to the narrow circle of its own conclusions; it sees nothing supernatural in the world; is deaf to those voiceless words, and blind to those invisible shapes which throng this universe. It disbelieves God's providence; doubts the truth of His holy Word; denies the personality, and with the personality, the personal and eternal love of God; nay, it even assails the being of the Deity, refining it away into an influence, a force, a law. And so one who was full of God in his youth, becomes pantheistic in his manhood; and having lost his hold on a Being in whom he may trust, satisfied with nothing, and doubting everything, becomes atheistic in his old age.

Who can speak without awe of a soul that has thus drifted from the anchor of its hopes, and has lost the clue to its high destiny? It roams aimlessly about the world, the prey of fate, or the sport of chance, making either a god of itself, or of the things of sense; with no certain

[a] 2 Pet. ii. 1, 9.

light on its present, no hope on its future. And paradoxical as it may seem, the mind that has thus "made shipwreck of faith," is apt, in order to satisfy its still yearning spiritual longings, to embrace the wildest delusions, and to become the prey of distempered imaginings, the profanities of spiritualism, or even the degrading arts of sorcery. And so it falls under the solemn condemnation of those who are abandoned to themselves: "Behold, all ye that kindle a fire, that compass yourselves about with sparks : walk in the light of your fire, and in the sparks that ye have kindled. This shall ye have at mine hand; ye shall lie down in sorrow [b]."

3. And there remains the third and last state in this decline and fall of the soul, when the will is gained over and overpowered, and enslaved by the same spirit of ill. In that mysterious element of our being—the will, lies the root of *character;* it is that movement of the soul that precedes act, and is inseparable from it; it is the parent of presumptuous sins, and when opposed to the Divine will, it sets the man in opposition to his Maker. It is the centre, therefore, of each man's active life, upon which all the future issues of his conduct depend, and by which the character of each act is determined. When that is corrupted, bribed, and perverted, the case seems to be hopeless. The heinousness of Saul's transgression, though seemingly of no flagrant type, lay in this; the guilt of Balaam, though he professed a readiness to obey the word of the Lord, lay in this; for he "loved the wages of unrighteousness," and would not be stopped in the pursuit of them ; while the active energy towards ill which it implies, is the very characteristic of the apostate angels. This perversion, then, and subjuga-

[b] Isa. l. 11.

tion of the will demands our most careful, prayerful concern. Watch it in its first spring and earliest activities. The choosing for oneself, where God has set a way before us; the neglect of some duties because homely or irksome, and choosing others; the selection of our own creed, because more agreeable to our own sentiments; the resistance of authority whether human or divine, because distasteful; every deliberate act of ill against the rebuke of conscience, and the remonstrances of friends,—these betoken that wilfulness of soul which is doing despite to the spirit of grace, and is gradually binding round it the fetters of Satan.

For we must observe in passing, two things; first, that this making our own will our rule and our master, is not a simple isolated act, but it is, more than this, resistance to a higher will, to the Spirit of God, which has been given to the Christian and is his rightful master, and which is thus done despite to, and driven away; and, secondly, that in thus choosing, we choose not freedom but bondage. How long is it ere we receive and embrace that divine lesson, that as each creature is only then free when it acts in accordance with the true laws of its existence, so the soul when led and guided by the Spirit who made it, is free, for "where the Spirit of the Lord is there is liberty;" that in resisting or shaking off this we but invoke upon ourselves and from within ourselves a force foreign to our true lives and highest interests, and become the slaves of self, the slaves of evil. How late alas! is this frequently learned, how hardly is that divine help which can unloose the bonds we have fastened upon ourselves regained! And when the downward course is fully run, and in addition to perverted affections, and darkened and deceived reason, there is joined the perversity of a rebellious will,

Sacred Scripture testifies over and over again, not merely to the possibility of a judicial reprobation, but to the unutterable misery of a soul thus abandoned of God, thus given over to perdition. It may be that the unhappy transgressor may be all unconscious of this; it may be that he congratulates himself on being his own master, and has no dread anticipations to harass him; but if it be so, it can only be because blindness has come upon him, the light that was within him is dark, the great transgression is close to him, if it have not already been consummated. Or, on the other hand, it may be that he is made to feel the misery that is gathering upon him, some lingering convictions torment him, and "a fearful looking for judgment" haunts him, but he is powerless to make an effort against it, and can only resist it in stubborn recklessness or gloomy despair; but in both cases, we cannot but recognise the reality of that state of reprobation which God's Word not unfrequently and not obscurely indicates as possible, whether or not it be denoted by the "unpardonable sin," or "the sin unto death," and as characterizing those who ere their earthly sun has set, have plunged themselves into the darkness and slavery of spiritual abandonment.

This is indeed a sad and painful subject. Yet it is well to contemplate it at times, to know the susceptibilities of the soul, and the subtlety and power of its adversaries, and thus to arrest the careless, even at the risk of alarming the timid and the anxious.

Not for a moment do I suppose that any one here present has reached or is reaching this fatal end to his career. Nor can we ever cease to tell each living soul that there is no sin so deep but that the blood of our redeeming Lord can blot it out for the penitent, no conscious state of spiritual infirmity which the Holy Spirit cannot and will not repair and fortify. But it is to prevent such a state, to deter from these sins that bring it on; to awaken self-examination; to save from coldness, indifference, and a creeping spirit of unbelief; to lay bare in some way "the powers of the world to come," to pluck back those (if there be such) who haply may be setting their foot within the shadow of that fatal tree, beneath whose branches those who slumber, slumber the sleep of death, that Lent and its exercises are ordained. For this end may they be blest to us. May the Lord strengthen and preserve us; if falling, may He restore us ere we have fallen far; and call us back, while yet within hearing of His gracious voice, to the light we are forsaking, and to the Shepherd from whom we have gone astray.

SERMON VII.

Aids in the Conflict:—God's Gifts of Grace.

HEBREWS iv. 16.

"Let us come boldly unto the throne of grace, that we may obtain mercy, and find grace to help in time of need."

IN the order of subjects which has guided your thoughts through the special sermons of this season, you have already passed over what is most difficult: it is the easier part of our meditation which lies before us now. What seemed most hard, and most urgent too, was to believe the presence of the enemy, the greatness of the peril; once thoroughly alarmed, we cannot but seek for help. It is when men doubt of Satan's power, or hold it cheap, that their spiritual state is worst. I have heard of a rich man who was entertaining his friends at a banquet, when one of his attendants whispered to him, that the house was on fire. "Put it out," was the careless reply; the guests were unconscious of their danger, and the feast went on. After a time the servant returned with the tidings that still the fire increased, but only to hear from his master the same command, repeated with more impatience at what he deemed a needless interruption of his pleasure. And so the wine-cup passed, and the mirth of the banquet grew higher;—until the third warning came, and the affrighted guests could but just escape with their lives from the conflagration around them: the house was destroyed. There are souls so deeply engrossed with the enjoyment of the world's good things, that no testimony will convince them of their danger; you cannot persuade them to resist the devil, for they have never seriously regarded him as their foe.

To you, however, I am speaking to-night, as to those who have known their peril, and have understood the malice and subtlety of the enemy that assails their souls. You ask, 'How shall we resist? Who will give us aid in the conflict? We feel that we are weak; we know that our foe is strong: how can our weakness be made strong enough for the contest we have to wage?' It is well with you, Christian brethren, if your hearts have really asked such questions as these; if you have cried for help, because you knew that you were helpless in yourselves. The kingdom of heaven is for the poor in spirit,—for those who have so deeply felt the feebleness of their unaided power, and the failure of their best efforts, that they have formed a lowly estimate of themselves, and have learned humility from defeat. It is well with you, if you smart under the abiding memory of the wounds which sin and Satan have given you; well with you, if you "go softly all your years in the bitterness of your souls," remembering that you have been close to the gates of the grave, and that your own struggles were powerless to raise you in that time of distress. Anything is better than the false confidence which cheats a foolish heart with praise, and flatters only to betray.

Yet neither is this the state in which a Christian is to abide. The remembrance of past sins and failures is a condition of being restored, not restoration itself. To be for ever dwelling on past errors and present weakness, if it leads to nothing better, is but a distortion of the Christian character. A life all tears and sad confessions ill agrees with the portrait of the soldier fighting his good fight of faith, the runner winning his race, the husbandman toiling heartily in the vineyard with well-grounded hope of reward. The penitential sadness of Lent is, as many of you know, a blessed privilege; but Lent, after all, is only one short portion of the year: our annual round brings festivals, as well as fasts, to be observed. And even in this Lenten season it is well for you to be reminded that there are fruits of penitence, not in themselves of a sad complexion, which ought to spring from its due observance. If we are keeping it rightly, it is teaching us that we cannot do without a Saviour's help; and in the very process of teaching us, is disclosing to us something of that Saviour's love, and of our own well-grounded interest in its priceless gifts. The joy of finding deliverance, after we have known our danger and our need, is greater far than the happiness, such as it was, of vain security and ignorant guilt.

But *have* we found deliverance? Let the question be answered by a surer word than mine: "The Father ... hath delivered us from the power of darkness, and hath translated us into the kingdom of His dear Son." This is the Gospel of Christ, the burden of all preaching, the message so full of gladness and joy to us, that we forget its difficulties and its strictness, and in one comprehensive word call it all "good news." It is no mere hope or promise that it declared to us; the ambassadors of Christ proclaim an accomplished fact. St. Peter speaks indeed of one who has "forgotten that he was purged from his old sins;" but his thankless forgetfulness cannot alter the fact that he *was* purged once. We have passed into a new state, entered on another condition of spiritual life ;—rather, we have now begun to live, having before been as good as dead. I need not tell you with what earnest repetition, with what abounding thankfulness, the Scriptures speak of this new life; how they say that God hath quickened us, when we were dead, hath made us sit in heavenly places, hath created us anew, hath built us up for an habitation of God. With every variety of illustration, with accumulated force of assertion, they assure us that Satan hath been conquered, that the people of Christ are free.

But they will not suffer us to forget that it is only because we *are Christ's* people that this freedom is ours. Our life and liberty, our gifts and graces, all are traced to Him. "I am come," He said Himself, "that they might have life, and that they might have it more abundantly." And in the Epistle from which the text comes, the whole teaching of the Apostle leads us to dwell on the thought that far above us, at the right hand of the Majesty on high, we have a glorified High Priest, by one nature our brother, by another our God ; and that from that great High Priest, in virtue of His one sacrifice and of His perpetual mediation, all our strength and all our support are drawn. These are not the fancies of dreamy philosophers; they are the sober statements of men who lived by that faith of the Son of God which they professed, aye, and died for it too. They were not deceived—they have not deceived us— when they testified of a power from above which they felt and exercised, of a strength that was stronger than all the might of their spiritual foe, of a presence which did not fail them in the fiery hour of persecution, which did not desert them in the stormy conflict with worse enemies within.

Whatever this help was, no one, I suppose, will contend that we need it less than it was needed by apostles and saints. If they could not trust themselves, much more would it be presumptuous folly in us to lean on an arm of flesh. The graces which have been purchased for poor human nature by its union with the divine nature in the Person of Christ, are all *we* have to rely on in our conflict with those powers of darkness, who, though quelled, are not (we know too well) destroyed. Of our personal interest in that purchase, thanks be to God, there is no doubt. We are "every one members in particular" of Christ. From Him, as the Head, "all the body by joints and bands having nourishment ministered, and knit together, increaseth with the increase of God." Specially in the Sacraments, which make us partakers of Him, is that nourishment ministered, that union with Him cemented and maintained. The acts of faith in Him which we make, when we receive them, have promises of special returns of grace: their gifts and consolations are attested by the blessed experience of the people of Christ, who have been numbered with His saints, generation after generation, these eighteen hundred years. The Church has no richer treasures entrusted to her keeping than these.

Is it necessary to state these things to Christians of full age? If it is, does not the very necessity convey a reproach? It was right indeed that the Apostles should preach to Jews and heathens the unsearchable riches of Christ, of which they had never heard; but surely the tradition of Christian education must be weak, and the apprehension of Christian faith be feeble, if it is really needful to state again and again what great things our Master has done for us, what wealth of grace He has assigned for our use. "Let us come boldly," saith the Scripture; *we* come like timid strangers, doubting of our welcome, or uncertain of the nature of the prize we hope to win. We do not take in the extent of the mercy we have received, nor assure ourselves that it is really ours. It is one sad instance of this feeble faith, that thousands of Christian people are afraid, or profess to be afraid, to communicate at Christ's holy Feast. They cannot persuade themselves that *they* are really bidden, that grace is there pledged to *them*, that comfort, peace, and strength, are absolutely assured to *them* in the right receiving of that Holy Communion. It is another mournful instance, that so many doubt Christ's love to little children, and cannot persuade themselves that when He calls them to Him, He really means to adopt them as His own. So it is again with Confirmation, from which parents hold back their children, as doubting whether it can be true that God will really bless the young with His high gifts of grace. And in general, of our use of what are called the "means of grace," it may be too truly affirmed, that few come to them with the glad confidence of men who know their Master and His gifts. "Whatsoever we ask," says the Apostle, "we *know* that we have the petitions we desired of Him ;" and this assurance, strong in every act of prayer, should be stronger still in the reception of those Sacraments which have their own special grace annexed to the receiving of them in faith. But we seem to regard the ordinances of Christ as David regarded the armour of Saul, when he was going forth to meet the Philistine champion in fight. We put them aside with misgivings, and say "we have not proved them; we cannot go with these." David was right, for he had no warrant from God for believing that success should wait upon the use of royal weapons; past experience and inward inspirations told him that he might depend, by the mercy of God, on his shepherd's sling. *We have* a panoply, "the whole armour of God," ready for our wearing, blessed by its divine Giver; what defence can we hope to find, if we cast this away? I do not deny that there is a temptation to seek other defences; it is natural to rely on resources that seem to be within our own control. The stedfast purpose of a resolute will, the energy of a well-trained mind, manly courage, dignified self-respect, a lofty sense of honour, or a daring love of unselfish enterprise,—are not these great qualities? Can we not succeed by using such helps as these? Nay, brethren, but these are not helps at all; they are no additions to our resources; they are but parts of ourselves. And this is the very reason why we take delight in them. It pleases us to draw the picture of a self-reliant, self-supporting character, complete in itself, overcoming evil by its stern determination to do right. But it is a picture, and nothing more; it is founded on no reality, has no basis of fact whereon to rest. For our real condition, at all events since the Fall, has been one of dependence on a power above us. Something external to our own tainted nature, distinct from us, and separate from our sin, was needed to raise us when we had fallen. Therefore was the Son of God incarnate, that He might bestow on our nature what it could not gain for itself. He came to save sinners, because they could not save themselves. And, as man could not raise himself when he was fallen, so neither can he sustain himself in strength and spiritual health without grace. They have tried to do it,—the wise, the learned, and the great, the foremost nations, and the brightest ages in the world's history; and defeat, absolute defeat, is written on the memory of their attempts. We must have, —the noblest and meanest alike,—constant correspondence with the Author of that good which we cannot create; we must be in perpetual communication with One who bestows upon us from without what from within we cannot obtain. Does this seem a disappointing and disparaging estimate of life? The enemy of our souls would willingly have us think so. He would persuade us that it is better to be independent and sufficient for our own wants, that it is unworthy to be always looking to another for help. Men of high intellect and of powerful minds are not unfrequently taken by his snare. But surely, brethren, dependence is a noble thing, if it links us to a nature higher than our own. It was never thought unworthy, even amongst ourselves, to own submission to a worthy leader; the soldier follows an heroic chief, the student sits at the feet of a revered teacher, and it does but add to their reputation that they have stood in close relationship to the great and good. How much more when it is a question of communion with a higher nature than our own.

And this it is, which we mean by the dependence of the Christian soul on its God. It is a perpetual converse with the high and holy One, who is by that converse changing the soul more and more into His own likeness. It is a power of coming to Him at all times of need, and finding the very grace required for each conflict or distress. It is the privilege of admission to a presence-chamber, where the golden sceptre is always held out, and no prayer sent back unanswered or unobserved. Feelings and aspirations go up from the child of God perpetually to his Father in heaven, to be blessed with returns of grace that quicken those feelings into a new and still more blessed energy of love. But especially in acts of sacramental communion with his Lord does the Christian gather up and concentrate the powers of his lifelong communion with heaven. Then it is that he has most vivid impressions of the nearness of God to his soul, most comfortable assurance of strength for his need. At no time, indeed, is the mercy-seat withdrawn from his approach; but then it has a glory not granted to his ordinary gaze; the cloud from heaven rests upon it, and the faithful worshipper seems almost to pass behind the cloud, and exchange the weariness of earth for heaven itself.

There are some, I know, who would not speak of sacraments thus. To them they are weak and beggarly elements, too visible and material for the pure, spiritual life. If it were so, yet the humble penitent might perhaps deem that weak and beggarly elements best suited poor weak suppliants, such as he feels himself to be. But what right have we to use such words as these? Surely this is a thankless and unfilial criticism of our merciful Father's gifts. In the beginning our life was linked to heaven by a golden chain: man in his folly and self-will severed that bond of union; and God, of His dear love, has taken the shattered fragments and re-united us to Himself. If in restoring the bond between heaven and earth, He has left some visible pledges and tokens of His favour, if He has given us not words and thoughts only, but acts of devotion and outward sacraments of grace, should not our hearts see here a fresh proof of His wondrous pity for our infirmities, a new argument of His boundless love?

Alas! we do not reflect how much He has done for us, we do not see what great things He has put within our reach. Just consider what a story of triumph and success the Christian's life might be, if he were faithful to the grace bestowed on him. What an epitaph might be written on his tomb! It would tell indeed of temptations, but of temptations baffled and overcome; of sorrows, but of sorrows borne with meek patience and loving trust; of doubts and difficulties, but of difficulties that were habitually laid open in prayer to a heavenly Guide who never failed to resolve them; of infirmities, but of infirmities which in the very struggle to subdue them, brought new strength and hope to the faithful heart. What deeds of charity, what words of thoughtful wisdom, what services to Christ and His Church, would such a chronicle record! Turn and see what Christian biographies are now. I do not mean what they are as written by the hand of partial friendship, bound by its own amiable, but worthless, rule to say nothing but good of those whom it describes: I mean the biography contained in the pages of the unerring book, that faithfully records each word, and thought, and deed, as they have passed before the all-seeing eye of God. Such a biography there will be, nay there is, of each one among us. What, think you, if you could read it, would it say of you? It might speak perhaps of broken resolutions, and purposes that came to nought, of opportunities idly wasted, of foolish companions and misspent time, of prayers omitted or spoiled by distraction of thought, of unworthy communions, and of graces thrown away. It might describe a life that bore small tokens of usefulness on earth, few signs of earnest preparation for heaven. How grievous to reflect that, side by side with the record of such failure in the spiritual life, it must be declared that there was abundant provision for better things, divine resources that, if used in faith, must have ensured success.

I have brought you back to penitential thoughts, as perhaps on such a day as this it was meet to do. We have been meditating on the mercy of God, His ceaseless guidance of our lives, His never-failing gifts of grace for help in time of need. Let us go home, and think over them yet again. God forgive us, that we have thought of them so little, and used them so ill!

SERMON VIII.

Aids in the Conflict:—God's heavenly Host.

PSALM xci. 12.

"He shall give His angels charge over thee, to keep thee in all thy ways."

IT would be an inadequate description of the Holy Scriptures, to say that they are a revelation concerning God and man. They are as truly a revelation concerning the Angels. And this not merely indirectly, as the Angels are connected with us, but directly as to themselves, irrespectively of us. The original contest between the good and evil angels,—the difference as to the present condition of the one portion of the heavenly host, who "kept their first estate," and of the others who fell,—the consequent future destiny of Satan and his angels who were cast out, and are reserved for everlasting punishment in the Judgment of the Great Day; and on the other hand, of the faithful, who now glorious in bliss, will hereafter be raised together with redeemed man to a yet higher state, through the glory of the Incarnate Son, because it is the purpose of God, "in Him to reconcile all things to Himself, whether they be things on earth, or things in heaven[a];"—these main facts of their history are clearly revealed to us.

It has been attempted to resolve angelic appearances into mere subjective visions of the mind itself, illusory forms projected by the heated and devout imagination,

[a] Coloss. i. 20.

through its own creative agency; or to account for them objectively, by the supposition of the Divine power giving mere temporary visible shapes to a Divine message, forming a kind of phantasmagoria of an inner world, produced for the occasion, in order to impress the outward sense more vividly than by mere words.

That we are indeed entirely unable to explain how the Angels' spiritual bodies (for bodies of some refined subtlety they have ever been supposed to possess) can be adapted to human organs of sight; that we can form no real idea even of such a possibility,—is evident. But it would be unreasonable to doubt the possibility of God causing them, as He will, to appear to whom He will; or to give power to human eyes to discern their more subtle forms; imparting temporary visibility to what ordinarily would be invisible. And surely the attempt to explain these mysterious appearances on the theory of subjective ideas, or temporary phantom shapes, is wholly forced, is simply to take Holy Scripture in a nonnatural sense, and is unphilosophical, as being manifestly inadequate to account for the undeniable phenomena of the case.

For it is not merely the appearance of Angels to prophets and seers in ecstasy; not merely the occurrence of their presence in the poetical books of Scripture; not merely communications from God to the mind of lonely watchers and meditative hermits, such as the forms arrayed in gorgeous light and awful grandeur, which appeared to Daniel when he prostrated himself, and fell as one dead, on the banks of "the river Ulai," for which we have to account. The visits of Angels are described equally in prosaic historical books. Nothing can be more naturally interwoven with the ordinary narrative of common events, than a great proportion of the angelic appearances recorded in the Old Scriptures, such as the angel that appeared to Hagar in the wilderness, or the two who went down to Sodom to rescue Lot, and destroy those doomed cities, or the angel that met Balaam by the way.

Nor were these appearances visible merely at particular crises, as e.g. times of religious excitement, when men are specially open to dream dreams, and indulge in exaggerations of idea, and visionary conceptions; or periods of darker intelligence, when men are more specially subject to hallucinations and superstitious belief as to invisible presences. The appearances of angels extend throughout the Scriptures. They people the scenes of the sacred history, indeed, more fully at one period of man's history than another; but only with such differences as are readily accounted for by the more or less urgent call for Divine interpositions, or the greater or less prominence with which the designs of God required to be impressed on the minds of His people. With such exceptions there is little difference to be discerned. Angels are not more clearly seen around the gates of Paradise, at the beginning of man's history, than they are represented as about to be present at its close, on the day of the final resurrection and universal judgment. They are as fully concerned with the events of the Revelations of St. John, as they are with the events of the Book of Genesis. The Scripture history of mankind opens with the Angels already on the stage of this lower world, actively engaged. It is revealed that they will be as actively at work, when it has run out its predestined course. The Angels indeed group themselves in greater apparent numbers, and seem more intensely employed at certain great crises of our history, as e.g. on Mount Sinai, during the delivery of the Law, or during the earthly life of the Incarnate God. But the simplest view of Scripture assures us, that from the earliest to the latest epoch of man's destiny, these blessed and glorious beings have a co-ordinate and co-extensive part to play on the same stage of life, in which our own lot and probation are cast.

Moreover, this connexion between the Angels and men is not a mere casual or extraordinary interposition with human affairs, but is evidently an uniform appointment ordered and maintained on a settled plan. Their movements are not mere accidents of our state. To take first the lowest form of their ministration, they are represented as the active agents of the laws of matter, which so closely affect us. They inflict or save from death, as in Egypt during the Exodus. They cause or remove pestilences, as in David's history. They bind or unloose the winds, as in the Revelations. They have even yet more intimate and closer relation with the bodies of men. The "thorn in the flesh," of St. Paul, was "a messenger of Satan to buffet him[b]." The whole case of demoniacs is a familiar instance of this most mysterious intermingling of angelic powers with the secret constitution of man's physical nature. They act of course only under the guiding and restraining Will of God. They are subject wholly to His law. But they are as truly personal agents in the disposition of the subtle organizations and operations of His material kingdoms, within their sphere of power, and are as energetically at work around and within us, as we can be in our own sphere.

The Angels enter, which is still more important to us, into the moral order of the government of mankind. They direct and overrule with their powerful influences

[b] 2 Cor. xii. 7.

the life of nations. There was the prince or Angel of the kingdom of Persia[c], equally as the chief of all the good angels, St. Michael, was the watchful guardian of the chosen people of Israel. They entered also into family life; directing its most private concerns. Instances of this latter kind of interposition of Angels is seen in the history of the patriarchs, as in the marriage of Abraham's son, and in the protection of Jacob from his brother's anger.

Consider, then, at how many points of our merely natural state the angelic natures and powers affect us, —in the operations of material nature, in the moral government of the world, in our home life. These are what may be called the natural and ordinary intertwinings of the angelic order of being with that of man.

But what touches us more deeply, more closely far, is the energy of angelic ministrations in our supernatural state. This necessarily affects them as it affects us, in the more intense and momentous issues of life. Throughout the Old Testament there are indications of a constant struggle being maintained on behalf of God's elect by the good Angels, who are in constant conflict with the evil angels. On the one side, the side of the evil, there is the constant effort not merely to turn the forces of nature against man, and thus bring calamities upon him, but also to assault him in his inner life, to ruin his spiritual hopes, and mar for ever his glorious destiny. On the other side, the side of the good Angels, there is equally a constant counter-plotting, and earnest antagonistic strife, to maintain the struggling faithful among men, to ward off evil from them, to direct all events to their good, to guide, console, empower, animate them, never leaving them, till their mission of

[c] Dan. x. 13.

loving sympathy and constant interposition has fulfilled its predestined end.

The indications which the Book of Job gives in regard to the malice of Satan, and the watchful love of St. Michael in preserving the body of Moses, as an instance of similar zeal on the part of the good,—these can hardly be understood but as instances of a law, revelations coming out to view because of special circumstances, but really an interpretation of the inner history of the progress of events in the unseen world, which must from its very nature be going on unceasingly.

For the history of Job is manifestly intended as an encouragement to every one struggling under the oppression of trials of which he cannot perceive the justice, or the motive, though resolved to cling in trust upon God alone. It interprets for such sufferers the causes and forces at work in the supernatural world, with the assurance that they are all subject to the immediate direction and control of God, and can issue only in confusion to the ministers of evil, and the greater glory of those who abide faithful in the trial. It has an universal application, and consequently the agencies at work must equally be supposed to be universal. Similarly with the history of Moses. He was a representative person; representative of the elect people of Israel. His life was to be an example of a like faith with his own, to all who followed him. The tokens of God's love to him were assurances to them of His protection; the care which watched over him a sign of like care for them. The Guardian Angel of their leader, was to be the watchful ministrant also of God's love to the people whom he led.

But more especially we can discern, through the outward veil, the thrill and glow which has ever pervaded the holy Angels in fulfilling the charge committed to them in the gradual developing of the Incarnation of God. Their intense watchfulness to penetrate the secret; their earnest care of those more favoured ones who were preparing the way, as types or forerunners of the Advent of Jesus, as specially shewn in the family life of Abraham and Jacob; and then the ecstasy of angelic song which heralded the Nativity of Christ, and their composed, reverent eagerness as they watched around the Sepulchre; and ever afterwards the fervent action of the Angels moving with and around our Lord, in the heavenly order of His life subsequent to His Ascension, of which the visions of St. John speak; and on earth their "joy over one sinner that repenteth," their care of "the little ones" of Christ, and their last office of love to the departing souls of the elect "carried by the Angels" into Paradise,—these revealed representations of their concern in man, thus more constantly and more energetically stirred, prove that a new spring of life and love toward man had been imparted to the angelic natures in union with the Incarnation of God. They are quickened in themselves to a more vivid joy, a more glowing adoration, a more fervent charity towards man as the object of Divine care in Christ; bound to a dearer, more absorbing care, because of the tabernacling of God in human flesh.

The promise given to Nathanael, as the type of the true Israelite, that he should see "the Angels of God ascending and descending upon the Son of Man[d]," seems to speak of this new order of angelic agency; so new, that language is used by our Lord which at first sight implies that not till then had the interposition of Angels really commenced; that only then the heavens

[d] St. John i. 51.

would be opened, and the descent and ascent of Angels begin. In using the term, "Son of Man," in connexion with that promise—a term which always implies our Lord's human relation to His elect—He includes His elect of all times with Himself, as being thus destined to be more nearly related to the angel host, more specially objects of a fresh development of their care and love.

And certainly a very marked difference is to be discerned between the angelic ministrations of the older time, and those of the new dispensation. During the olden time the action of Angels, as revealed to us, was on a large scale, affecting the concerns of nations and kingdoms, and of families only inasmuch as the elect race was confined to a family, the patriarchal line through which the Messiah was to come. But nothing is said in the Old Testament of the individuality of the Angels' care; of it extending to all the elect; of a special relation of Angels to individuals, because of their individual relation to God; of such an extent of angelic ministrations, as would bring them home to every man's private and personal consciousness, as his own special support and joy. There were indications, no doubt, partial illustrations, of such a law in the Old Testament, but they are rare and exceptional. To look at the Old Testament only, one would have said that angel guardianship, and angels' secret communion, was reserved as the privilege of great typical personages, as patriarchs or prophets, or of great collective hosts of the elect people, but not of an elect soul as such; nor, if an Angel were an occasional visitant in any case, that he could, so to speak, be depended on as a constant companion, a sure ministrant of divine love and care at all times, "in all our ways."

This new and most eventful truth is one great distinguishing feature of the revelations of angel life in the New, as contrasted with those of the Old Testament. There for the first time we hear our Blessed Lord speaking of all His members, all His little ones, and saying that their "Angels do always behold the face of" His "Father, which is in heaven [e]." The words assert this great truth of one equally as of another. His Apostle unfolds yet further this great revelation, when he says that the Angels are "ministering spirits, sent forth to minister for them who shall be heirs of salvation [f];" language which equally includes all alike, all as "heirs," therefore without personal distinction. And the same Apostle asserts the same universality of individual privilege, when, speaking alike to all to whom his epistles are addressed, he says, "*Ye* are come unto Mount Sion, and unto the city of the living God, the heavenly Jerusalem, and to an innumerable company of Angels [g]."

The Church's traditional faith has been grounded on these pregnant passages. On these momentous words rests the belief of the guardian Angels of baptized souls, —of the daily care, the watchful protection, the ceaseless countless ministries of love and power, which are around every child of God's eternal adoption. This faith has grown out of these precious words of Jesus and His Apostles. They involved, therefore, a very marked change as to the faith regarding Angels; for there was revealed not merely a greater intenseness of interest and care, because of the greater momentousness of the charge of souls in whom God dwells, for whom God suffered and died, for whom the unceasing Sacrifice and intercession of the Lamb of God are being offered,—but the individuality of it, the like care extended to each, and its

[e] St. Matt. xviii. 10.   [f] Heb. i. 14.   [g] Ibid. xii. 22.

unceasingness from the font to the grave, through the grave to Paradise, and beyond Paradise to heaven. The Fathers drew out this great truth, always implying its intimate connexion with the Incarnation of God.

Thus Origen, addressing one of the elect, says, "Yesterday thou wast under a demon, to-day thou art under an angel. 'Do not,' says the Lord, 'despise one of these little ones who are in the Church; for verily I say unto you, their angels do always behold the face of My Father Which is in heaven.' Angels minister to their salvation; the sons of God have been granted to serve, and say unto each other, 'If He has descended with a body, if He hath been clothed in mortal flesh, and borne the cross, and died for men, why are we quiescent? Why spare we ourselves? Come, all ye angels, let us descend from heaven." Then, speaking of their individual care: "Come, O Angel! receive him who has been converted by the Word from former error, from the doctrine of demons, from iniquity speaking on high, and receiving him, like a good physician, cherish and instruct him[h].'" And St. Hilary says of their help to us in our prayers: "The authority is absolute, that Angels preside over the prayers of the faithful. Wherefore Angels daily offer up to God the prayers of those who are saved through Christ. Therefore is it dangerous to despise him, whose desire and supplications are borne to the eternal and invisible God by the holy service or ministry of Angels[i]." And again St. Ambrose speaks of their guarding even our inner hearts from the watchful foe: "Thus did Eliseus the prophet shew that armies of angels were around him as a defence; thus did Joshua recognise the leader of the heavenly host. They therefore who are able to fight for us, are able to guard the fruit that

[h] Hom. i. in Ezek.   [i] Tract. in Ps. cxxxiv.

is within us[j]." And again, St. Chrysostom connecting their ministering to us with that of our Blessed Lord's: "What marvel is it, if they (the Angels) minister to the Son, whenever they minister to our salvation? ... Yea, rather it is the work of Christ Himself, for He indeed saves as a Master, but they as servants [k]."

It is clear, then, that the belief has ever been a very practical one; and indeed how can we for a moment suppose that such an array of heavenly beings, so powerful, so ardent, so intense in action and love, can be, as they are sometimes regarded, the mere decorative features of a poetic religion, the beautiful imagery of the rapt moods of the devout mind?

Nor is it less sure that their aid is of the most intimate personal kind, although much mystery still hangs around the kind of communion which they are permitted to hold with us, and we have reverently to gather it by inference, rather than by direct revelation. It would seem that as a tendency "to the worshipping of Angels[l]" developed itself even in the apostolic age, possibly on this account a reserve was kept as to the greatness of our obligations to these blessed guardians, lest in the instruments and agents of the Divine care we should lose the constant sense of the supreme Author both of their and our life. Even St. John needed a warning to preserve in his mind the clear assurance, that notwithstanding all their greatness and their power to aid, they are but "fellow-servants [m]." But, if careful to take heed to such warnings, we may safely cherish for our stay and comfort, and in reverent regard to them for their kindness towards us, profound and earnest thoughts of their succour and defence which, according to the will of God, they never

[j] *De Virgini*, c. 8.   [k] Hom. iii. in Ep. ad Heb.   [l] Col. ii. 18.
[m] Rev. xxii. 9.

cease to supply to us in our need. Nor surely ought we to scruple to do so, when we see how our Lord Himself, compassed with our flesh, was behoven to an Angel's care, when creation saw the Eternal Son prostrate in His agony, and "an Angel strengthening Him ;" or when, after the temptation was past, Angels "came and ministered unto Him."

Or again, can we attribute to the holy Angels a less power to aid us, than is permitted to the evil angels to hurt us? Must not angelic instrumentality be at least equal on either side? We know indeed little of the laws which determine the action of spirit upon spirit; or of the communion and strengthening influence which one being can interchange with another; or how one soul can stay itself on another soul, and thought mingle with thought, love with love, desire with desire; or how the higher mind and more powerful will of one creature may rule and direct the mind and will of the less powerful creature. But the later books of Holy Scripture reveal to us startling facts as to the powers of evil spirits in exercising the most intimate control over, and holding closest communion with, the inner life of man. There we read of Satan establishing himself within the very soul of man, thus to sway and rule him. There we learn, that the evil angel is "the strong man armed keeping his palace" within man's innermost nature, spirit within spirit directing the faculties of the possessed soul to devilish purposes. These fearful descriptions imply varied modes of influencing the soul. They shew the possession of some secret subtle power in the evil spirit to suggest sin, inflame the imagination, excite the will, cloud the understanding, overrule and direct the energies, gradually leading captive the whole man, and impressing upon him his own likeness, so that men thus possessed become the very "children of the wicked one;" although wholly unlike the power of God in this, that the evil angels can do nothing within the man except with his own free compliance.

And is not this in all probability the perversion of a power intended to have been used for a true end; the fallen angels perverting to their own bad purposes a commission given to them, when they were in union with God, to use for God, and for the good of the other creatures of God?

And with this certain knowledge thus revealed to us of the influence of the evil angels, may we not conclude that no less power is being exercised by the unfallen Angels, who still delight to use it as God gave, and designed it; that the good Angels not merely surround us to contend for us against the assaults of the evil "principalities and powers," who would destroy us; not merely that they succour and defend us with their countless services of loving and watchful care to aid our weakness, or supply our need; but that also, in union with God, they influence our inner life, suggest holy thoughts, captivate our imaginations, stir our wills, illumine our understandings, aid our efforts, direct our energies, and holding secret communion of spirit with spirit, within our spirits, minister to us the gracious gifts of God? How such subordinate ministries are combined with the working of the All-holy Spirit Himself, we know not; yet in acknowledging the instrumentality of the lower agency we are not excluding Himself, the Source of power. We are rather the more reverencing our own manifold joys and assurances of support, even as in natural things we can delight in the lower instrumentalities of pleasant food, and sweet flowers, and genial light, while their beauty and pleasantness enhance the more, do not exclude, the blessed thought of God, Who gives and orders through their means all these good things of His natural providence. The invisible Angels are to us in the spiritual world, what the thousandfold ten thousand ministrations of visible creatures around us are in the natural world. We cannot indeed interchange sensible intercourse with the Angels that aid and defend us, but when their charge is fulfilled in bearing our souls to the Lord, we shall rejoice the more that we have believed the truth and love of God in ordaining for us their unseen agencies, even as we trusted to His innumerable visible agencies. Being made one with Christ, we share in and through Him what was His earthly joy, what cheered Him when the temptation was over, and sustained Him in His agony when He was weak, and Who meant the promise to be our blessing, as it was His own: "There shall no evil happen unto thee, neither shall any plague come nigh thy dwelling. For He shall give His angels charge over thee, to keep thee in all thy ways [n]."

Let us in conclusion lay to heart some practical lessons, which we may apply to our personal life.

Here first we may see the greatness and dignity of our position, our intended lot. Our mission in the world is, together with the holy Angels, and through their aid, to uphold the cause of God against the evil powers which oppose Him; to contend earnestly against whatever He has condemned; to be jealous of His honour; to be zealous of His commands. This was man's original call when, taken from the earth, he was placed, not as his first position, but by grace, in the garden of

[n] Ps. xci. 10, 11.

Eden °, with Angels as his companions, to "keep it" for God, against the evil which then assailed it. Man failed, and fell. But the call, and the power to fulfil the call, was without repentance, and is revived again in Christ. In our blessed Lord, our true representative, in the wilderness of temptation, ministered to by Angels, and assaulted by Satan, we see the renewed man, we see our own present lot. Surrounded on all sides by what tempts the eye, deceives the heart, captivates the senses, bewilders the understanding, shakes the faith, the loyalty, the allegiance, the stedfastness, of our frail nature, we are subjected to our course of trial. But Angels are at our side, and God above, around, beneath, within us, to uphold, to fortify, to preserve us, if only with His words in our lips, and His will in our hearts, we stand firm, and "resist the devil," till he "flee from us." Placed thus we are in this lower world, as having dominion over the creatures, and as the representative of the God-Man, to keep ourselves pure; to be strong for the truth and love, the beauty and the glory of a higher world; to resist "the lust of the flesh, and the lust of the eyes, and the pride of life, which are not of the Father, but which are of the world P." While we have the confidence, as we trust to our Lord, that He will sustain us, as He sustained Himself, because we are His, we have the assurance also that we are not merely surrounded by visible objects, but that we dwell in the midst of an invisible world, a world of most energetic and glorious life, a world of spiritual beings, in comparison with whom we are "made a little lower"

° "The Lord God formed man of the dust of the ground. .... And the Lord God planted a garden in Eden; and there He *put the man* whom He had formed. .... And the Lord God *took the man*, and put him in the garden of Eden to dress it and to *keep* it."—(Gen. ii. 7, 8, 15.)

P 1 St. John ii. 16.

for awhile, that at last we may be raised above them, when all things shall be put under our feet, because Christ is so raised, and we are of Him, and in Him, nearest to His throne, fellow-heirs of His glory.

Thus girt about with Angels, we are set to keep the charge of God. They are with us by our altars in the Mysteries. They are with us as we kneel in prayer. They are with us in the dangers of our way to keep us. They are by our beds to watch near us as we sleep, continuing by our side the adoration of the ever-present God in which we fell asleep. While we bear in our heart the consciousness of the Presence in which "we live, and move, and have our being," and of the heavenly hosts around us, shall we not be strong to resist temptation? Shall we do deeds from which good Angels must turn away in horror? Shall we speak words which they will repeat in heaven, and write down against us? Shall we bear on our countenances a look of malice, or impurity, or scorn, at which they must stand aghast? Shall we nourish in our hearts a thought from which they will turn away and weep? Shall we continue in sin, till our life's destiny is reversed, and we are again become more fit to be under a demon's, than an Angel's, care?

Or if after sin we return to God, when we fear again the power of Satan over us, and tremble at his temptations, and the return of his assaults, and the subtlety of his approach; or even doubt anxiously whether it may even yet be, that "after the sop," the love of Christ again rejected, we should be doomed and given up, reprobate; and Satan entering into oneself as his merited prey, we be cast out to be with him for ever, we may derive comfort and assurance from the thought that a greater spiritual power in the strength of God, ever at war with the rebel angels, and sent specially to minister to those who trust in Christ, are encamped around us, are guarding us, and will fight for us, driving away the tempter. Or if we feel shame before our brethren because of our past sins, and think that all eyes look on us with reproach, and that we can scarce venture into the presence of the pure, that none can believe our conversion; and we are weak, because of this sense of distrust or degradation which haunts us,—we may turn away and take refuge in the fellowship of Angels who are all the while rejoicing over the "one sinner that repenteth," with whom all thought is absorbed in the one deep love and thanksgiving, which is being breathed into them out of the Heart of Jesus, Whose grace has at last won the victory.

We are on our probation; and the history of the Angels is a warning which leaves no hope, if the hour of our probation pass, and we are found unfaithful. Of kindred natures with our own, the first-born of the creation of God, free to stand, or free to fall, they were subjected to trial, and by trial their everlasting state has been fixed. This law, ordained for the higher orders of the creatures of God, has found its sure fulfilment in their destinies. If they who fell from their high estate, escaped not, and all their greatness and endowments of grace availed not to exempt them from the consequences of the law of their creation, how can we look to escape a similar fate, if we fail by a like faithlessness? If we miss the day of our probation, faithless found among the faithful, unconformed to the will of God, not having served Him acceptably according to His purpose, —if our salvation is the hard-won purchase of the amazing Sacrifice of the cross, the passion, and death of the

Son of God,—and to carry on and complete His work of love, His Spirit's abiding Presence has been mercifully shed forth into our hearts, and, as our guard and aid in our warfare, the Angel host is sent to minister to us,—and yet we fail to work out this great salvation, and so great love and care be all in vain,—what must be reserved for us in the Great Day, when God shall arise to judgment, and he only that hath endured faithful unto the end, shall be saved?

As the Angels who kept their first estate, are our sure aids in our conflict, even so the fallen angels, who are reserved in everlasting chains under darkness, are a sure warning, that the condemnation which has already been visited upon them, will reach us also; and this the more certainly if, with their example before us, we continue in sin, sharing their disobedience,—which may God in His infinite mercy avert for His dear Son's sake, Jesus Christ our Lord, to Whom, with the Father, and the Holy Ghost, be all glory and thanksgiving for ever. Amen.

SERMON IX.

Aids in the Conflict:—The Communion of Saints.

ST. JOHN vi. 57.

"He that eateth Me, even he shall live by Me."

THERE can be no doubt that we have fallen back in many things from the simplicity of the primitive type, in our Christian course. But in nothing, perhaps, more manifestly than in our general view of the necessity of receiving the Holy Communion; of its place in our worship; of its effectual help to us in our conflict with the adversary; of its comfort under bereavements, trials, losses; of its sanctifying effect and power in all the passages of life; and above all, of its intimate connection with that holy doctrine which, but for the express mention of it in the Creed, must have faded out of the remembrance of many,—the doctrine of the communion of saints. The receiving of the Lord's Supper has become—I might say it has degenerated into—an occasional effort to recover ourselves out of the snare of sin. Every now and then, by preparation for the Holy Communion, men think to alter their course, which is setting too much towards the world, in a direction heavenward. If you well consider the matter, for I do not wish to overstate anything, (that would frustrate my speaking to you,) it has come to this with many, if not most professing Christians, that they receive the Lord's Supper more frequently—out of its due time as it were—if there be a predisposing sorrow, and when that is past, return to the ordinary infrequency; and with most, the infrequency is very great; so that the words we are considering, as regards any actual application to our daily life, lose all that force which they would plainly have if our partaking of the Body and Blood of Christ in the Lord's Supper was of the nature of a habit. That our Lord designed it to be a habitual receiving, no man can possibly doubt who considers His own words in the institution, as they were understood by those who heard them. They certainly continued as stedfastly in the breaking of bread as they did in prayers. The shadowing out of the mystery in the words of the text points in the same direction. In fact, nothing but the practice of men whom we know, and live and converse with, and whose whole life and conversation has necessarily an effect upon our own, nothing but stern fact, and the preconception which custom brings with it, could possibly make us think for one moment that a man was in any kind of safety who gathered himself up at Easter to perform the annual commemorative act sacramental, and then gave it up for a year as a thing above his ordinary life, too high for the temptations incident to his calling. This arises out of a total misconception of the thing, of the institution, and the doctrine contained in it. The doctrine contained in it is precisely what our Lord meant when He said, "He that eateth Me, even he shall live by Me." He that is joined unto the Lord is one spirit with the Lord. But how shall we be joined unto Him? It is written, "By one Spirit we are all baptized into one Body, and have been all made to drink into one Spirit." And again, in the Epistle to the Hebrews, we are bidden to "draw near with a true heart, in full assurance of faith, having our hearts sprinkled from an evil conscience," (surely by His Blood, in whatever way He was pleased to communicate to us the benefits of His most precious blood shedding,) "and our bodies washed with pure water." This means, it can mean nothing else, that our union with Him is by these effectual sacramental signs of His own appointment, as it is expressed in our own Communion Service: "If with a true penitent heart and lively faith we receive that holy Sacrament, then we spiritually eat the Flesh of Christ and drink His Blood; then we dwell in Christ and Christ in us; we are one with Christ, and Christ with us."

All this is brought to nought by an infrequent, unwilling reception. The spirit of it is absolutely taken away. Our Church has afforded the utmost possible latitude in that rubric,—" Every parishioner shall communicate at least three times in a year;" meaning, as Bishop Beveridge justly observed, that unless a person communicate three times in the year the Church doth not judge him to be in a state to receive that holy mystery. To shrink from closeness of union with Christ is, if you will consider it, a sign either of indifference or of conscious wilful unfitness, through some sin committed knowingly, or state of sinfulness permitted, or omission of felt and acknowledged duty. To turn the receiving of the Holy Communion into an occasional effort to recover ourselves out of a state of worldliness in which we know we ought not to live, is entirely an imagination of our own concerning it. And however common it be (so common that a man might almost express surprise at such a received opinion being spoken against), however much it be the practice of men to use it thus, it is contrary, as I have shewn you, to the doctrine and spirit of our services, to the words of the Lord Himself, " He that eateth Me, even he shall live by Me."

Suffer me now, in confirmation of what has been said, to draw your attention to the place which the receiving of the Holy Communion occupies in our worship. After the Commandments read, in order that on hearing each part of God's law we may search our hearts and see if we are living by it,—after a prayer and reading of two short passages of Holy Scripture, the Epistle and Gospel, and saying with united voice one of our confessions of faith,—after an act of love or charity done during the reading of sentences from Scripture exhorting to that grace,—the priest is directed to lay on the holy table the alms for the poor, and other devotions of the people, and when there is a Communion, so much bread and wine as he shall think sufficient. How often there shall be a Communion the Church doth not order, except that in cathedral churches and colleges, where there are many priests and deacons, all shall receive Communion every Sunday at the least. Every Sunday at the least.

Therefore in large parishes, where there are many communicants (which are increased at every Confirmation by 200 or 300 more, capable at least of receiving), it may be right to provide for some to receive communion every Sunday, using the discretion which the Church places in our hands; for no word of monthly, or any other stated number of communions, is so much as named, except that if a parishioner doth not communicate thrice in a year he is under censure, as a priest or deacon in a cathedral is under censure who doth not communicate every Sunday. Now, brethren, how often soever, or how seldom soever, you communicate, you must remember that the whole of the Communion Service to which you listen every Lord's Day to the end of the offertory sentences, is your preparation for the receiving of the Lord's Supper. Whenever you hear those commandments you must try and measure your conscience by them. What swearer doth not inwardly tremble when he heareth " The Lord will not hold him guiltless that taketh His Name in vain?" What man who doeth nought for his father or mother, or setteth light by them, heareth the fifth commandment without a thought in his heart, " Am I free from blame here?" Doth not the prohibition to kill, to do uncleanness, to thieve, ever strike on some conscience? And so when it comes to the act of faith, especially its last solemn words, "I look for the resurrection of the dead, and the life of the world to come," have we not often thought within ourselves, as we uttered the words with our lips, " Alas, do I live, am I now living, as one who looks for such things?" All is to the same effect, to the purifying of the heart by faith as a preparation for that union with Christ in the Holy Sacrament. And then the sentences, exhorting us to remember the poor, and the preachers of the gospel, and the whole household of faith, are still designed to prepare us for the more pious, and loving, and cheerful partaking together of the Lord's Supper, whether then immediately or on some future day. For I do not mean that all are expected to partake always. I am only attempting to shew you that sometimes all should, and that the whole service is with a view to that one act of worship. I am only protesting against this grievous neglect that has crept in, this deadening doctrine of the world, that you live in Christ by the act of coming together to pray, and sing praises, and hear the Word, when He Himself hath said, " He that eateth Me, even he shall live by Me," and, breaking bread, bade His disciples do that thing in remembrance of Him. So that this became the practice of the first converts, to break bread together, even as they prayed together, so shewing forth their Lord's death in the cities where they dwelt. Now see how we have fallen back from the primitive type, as I said.

We have a conflict with an adversary of such power as the besieger of a city hath, when he hath in the city a strong party on his side. So is Satan with regard to every one of us. He besets us alway, and in every man's heart he hath some evil inclination, or affection, or desire on his side, and, if it were not for the help of One greater than he, he should utterly destroy every soul which he proceedeth to assault. Not one of us can stand against him, but by the help of our God. No man ever did vanquish him outright but one, and He was both God and man. But all His faithful followers He did so incorporate into Himself, by a mystical but real union, that they need not fear the tempter's power to kill. " He that eateth Me, even he shall live by Me." "The thief cometh not," He said, speaking of Satan, "but for to steal, and to kill, and to destroy. I am come that they might have life, and that they might have it more abundantly:" that they might eat and live; as their first parents ate and died, so they might eat of Me, the true Tree of Life, and live. Yes: over them that are in Christ by spiritual partaking of Him, Satan hath no power—no power, at least, to kill. Now you see, brethren, that in proportion to the closeness of the union with the Saviour, must be the safety from the assaults of the enemy. None of you can doubt that. And if the union with Him be in partaking of His Body and Blood, with a true penitent heart and lively faith, it being a spiritual act, then to partake often must be what is needful unto more assurance of help. The rule is, the oftener the better, if in faith, and penitence, and charity. We forfeit so much help in our conflict with the adversary, as we do communicate either less frequently, or more coldly and backwardly. But I said also that we had lost sight of its sanctifying effect and power in all the passages of life. So it is indeed. Not only is He, on whom we feed by faith, the strength, and joy, and salvation, of every individual soul, coming to Him in this holy ordinance as He hath commanded, but the communion of His Body and Blood is the strongest and holiest link which binds us together in Him. "For we being many are one bread and one body, for we are all partakers of that one bread." This, was to be in the place of those earthly relationships which Christ declared His coming should rather have a tendency at first to weaken and to dissolve, than to cement and strengthen. When father and mother should forsake a child, the Lord should take him up; henceforth he should be adopted into another family, another should be his father, even Christ. "That which we have seen and heard," writes St. John, i.e. the mystery of God and the Father, and of Christ,—" that which we have seen and heard declare we unto you, that ye also may have fellowship with us: and truly," he adds, "our fellowship is with the Father, and with His Son Jesus Christ." The Evangelist who wrote these words, was the same who records the last prayer of our Blessed Lord, in which He prayed "not for these alone, but for them also which should believe on Him through their word. That they all may be one, as Thou Father art in Me, and I in Thee, that they also may be one in Us." That prayer never faded from St. John's memory while he lived, and while he taught. "Little children, love one another," was his favourite precept to those

K

who came to inquire of Christ at his mouth. He has been called the Apostle of love from that circumstance; the loving, and the beloved. To him, as filled with the spirit of the new commandment, did our Lord on the cross commit the charge of His mother, when the sword of grief had pierced through her soul, "and from that hour that disciple took her unto his own home." In that household, from that very day, may have been seen the true type of the communion of saints. What a home that must have been, where every meal was consecrated by the remembrance of His last meal on earth with His disciples, and by the mystical words He spake, and the sign He instituted, and the commandment He gave, "This do in remembrance of Me." What if they ate often in haste, with their loins girded for some work of charity, or to escape for their life; what if they ate it with bitter herbs, in sorrow of heart for all the suffering they had witnessed, and which they could never forget; yet what a home of love, and what a sanctifying effect and power must their communion have had on all the passages of their life ever afterward. We are not told how the love which reigned in that house surpassed in breadth, and depth, and height the ordinary love of parent, children, brethren, friends; our eyes have not been permitted to gaze upon such a holy privacy; but we are sure that if ever the grace of God did overshadow any home, so that every thought, and word, and action reflected His image, into whose likeness they grew and were transformed day by day, it must have been there, in that house. There truly, if anywhere on earth, must the love of God have been perfected. And the nearest to this must be the house where every member of a Christian family, as one by one they come to years of discretion, becomes a communicant, and each, comprehending by degrees the mystery of Christ's indwelling by the force of an inward experience, fashions his daily life accordingly. Brethren, there are many such houses. We need not here say in our heart, "Who shall ascend into heaven" (that is, to bring down Christ from above), "or who shall descend into the deep?" (i.e. to bring up Christ again from the dead). "For the God and Father of our Lord Jesus Christ, of whom the whole family in heaven and earth is named, hath granted unto many, according to the riches of His glory, to be strengthened with might by His Spirit in the inner man; so that Christ dwelleth in their hearts by faith; and they, being rooted and grounded in love, have been able to comprehend with all saints what is the breadth, and length, and depth, and height, and to know the love of Christ, which passeth knowledge, so that they are filled, verily, with all the fulness of God."

In the great conflict which is raging, which is at our doors, which hath in it the verification of some of our Divine Master's and His Apostles' prophetic sayings, so that we know it to be the beginning of that very conflict which we are taught to expect,—in which a mans' foes should be they of his own household, in which members of the same family should take opposite sides, —which should be known by pride and selfishness, disobedience to parents, ingratitude, unholiness, want of natural affection, love of pleasure,—in fine, by a form of godliness without the power;—in the conflict in which the subtilty of this world's wisdom shall corrupt many minds from the simplicity that is in Christ, shall there be no refuges, whither a man may flee for help and comfort in the fiery trial; if one falleth, shall there be no one to lift him up? Oh yes! He said—our Divine Lord said— He would not leave us comfortless; He would come to us.

And surely He hath fulfilled His word. Wherever two or three are gathered together in His name, there is He in the midst of them. The glory which God gave Him in His human nature, He hath given them. What was that glory? "That they may be one, even as We are one, I in them and they in Me; that they may be made perfect in Me." This is that communion of saints, which is nourished and sustained by the Holy Communion of His Body and Blood. These refuges of which I spake are the homes and houses of God's saints; those helpers at hand and ready to succour us are men like-minded, having the same love, being of one accord, of one mind,— such men as Epaphras, Onesimus, Timothy, Tychichus, and others, who were St. Paul's fellow-workers unto the kingdom of God, which were a comfort to him in the dangers and distresses and necessities which he endured,—such persons as Priscilla and Aquila, who for his life laid down their own necks. Such men and such women there are yet in the world. And if our heart should ever fail us for the multitude of the adversaries, think, brethren, if our eyes were opened, and we saw the great cloud of witnesses who have gone before, the saints that are at rest, the spirits of the just made perfect, the glorious city where they and we shall dwell for ever and ever! But enough for us, that in us and our fellow-pilgrims, who are journeying at our side to the heavenly country, Christ dwelleth. Enough that He has said, "He that eateth Me, even he shall live by Me." Enough that, assembled together with our brethren, we feed, in a heavenly and spiritual manner, on the Body of the Lord, and drink His precious Blood. Enough that, so doing, we find ourselves strengthened for the trials of the day, and guided safely through the darkness of the night; and see far on before us the shining pinnacles of the holy city, whither He, whom we have adored and trusted in, and loved with all our hearts, is gone to prepare a place for us; not a mere refuge, as one thinks of the grave, where "the wicked cease from troubling, and the weary are at rest," but a place of joy and gladness, and unfading light for ever, and for evermore.

SERMON X.

The Weapons of our Warfare.

2 COR. x. 4.

" The weapons of our warfare are not carnal."

ROM. xii. 21.

" Overcome evil with good."

IF St. Paul is fond of reminding us of the militant character of the Christian life, it is he also who warns us oftenest of the danger of allowing the metaphor to lead us astray. He knew that there is that in our nature which responds readily to the trumpet-call. "To resist even unto blood," "to fight the good fight," "to quit ourselves like men," "to wrestle against principalities and powers;"—these, and suchlike figures, have a ring which carries them straight home to generous hearts. The poet surely has not painted falsely the chivalrous dreams of youth,—

"Waiting to strive a happy strife,
To war with falsehood to the knife."

Life seems to very many of us indeed a battle. We see selfishness and cowardice, and our blood boils at the sight of them. We see evil all about us, evil that might be prevented. We imagine ourselves in our day-dreams of the future, even in some small measure in our actual experience, to be bearing a part in the world-old conflict, in the war which "was in heaven." We are on the side of good. Does it not follow that what opposes us is on the side of ill? We know, indeed, and feel keenly, that the very evil which we are combating is in our own hearts also; the very frivolity, the very narrowness, the indolence that clings to what is, the deep irreverence of the heart, even in its germ and possibility the saddest moral corruption. We are conscious that the enemy is very near us, and our attitude towards it constrains us in some sort to live as becomes a knight of God. It lifts, and strengthens, and purifies us.

And yet there is a danger in all this. We need to hear often the Apostle's warning voice, " The weapons of our warfare are not carnal." Life is too complicated to be comprehended in one metaphor. It is a *battle*, in which one side must conquer and one must yield; it is a *race*, in which all may be crowned; it is a *field*, where good and bad grow together, and the tares may not be rooted up lest the wheat be rooted up with them. *It is a battle*, but how subtle, how unearthly is the conflict; how different from the coarse semblances which are all that meet our eyes! What a sad medley, what a strange inexplicable maze must any struggle between man and man, between two human causes, even between the visible Church and any cognisable power without her, appear to one who can read the spiritual issues of the strife! How often Trojan bears Greek arms, and the patriot's sword strikes to a brother's heart!

To make mistakes in history is a small matter. To reverence as the sole depositories of truth or goodness one person or one party in some bygone strife, may not inflict serious damage on our moral nature, for the objects of our reverence will have been first idealized. But it is no imaginary danger, especially in days of more than usual earnestness and difference, that we may be tempted to identify the cause of good, that cause which demands our love and our life, with the cause of some particular party, or of some particular movement, which we are at the moment supporting. For the good, for the truth, we may fight, we must fight, absolutely; there is no reserve, no doubt on the question. But this is a spiritual warfare. The enemy is no visible one, the weapons of no mortal forging. We wrestle not against flesh and blood, not against men like ourselves, with mixed natures, with minds which at the best but know in part, which at the worst are temples which the truth-revealing Spirit has not yet forsaken, but against spiritual powers, against that spirit of falsehood and unbelief which is within us as well as without us. But the questions on which we shall do battle with our fellow men seldom or never raise the issue simply between good and ill. They are questions of fact. "Is this good?" "Is this the truth?" "Is this a part and parcel of the faith once delivered?" There must be a right and a wrong on such questions; but if good and wise men differ, the probability is that neither of the contending parties has all the truth or all the error.

Shall we, then, stand aside and look on as with the irony of Epicurean gods, while men debate the great problems of God's nature and man's destiny? Shall we care nothing whether the doctrine in which our own soul has found peace and cleansing is offered to others in all its strength and purity? Nay, surely that would be to be false to the good we know, to the truth which we believe. But yet the thought of human fallibility, of the many-sidedness of truth, will soften and humble our bearing in controversy; it will make us ready and eager to recognise the good on our opponent's side. We shall drop at times the fierce metaphor which at the best has something in it that hardens, that narrows, that injures the bloom and modesty of a Christian soul. We shall no longer be fighting against our brethren for the truth, but following after, even as they, if that we may apprehend that which we have not yet apprehended; still seeking for the truth, even as they, though it may be from a different side.

"The weapons of our warfare are not carnal." Let us feel this really, and we may safely use the image which the Apostle thus completes and guards. It is indeed a noble image of the Christian life,—the image of the faery knight, "too simple and too true" to pass unscathed through the treachery of the world, but triumphant at the last, because he "strives for the right," and "the good is God's,"—the image of the "happy warrior," such as even in earthly warfare the Christian poet paints him,—

> " The generous spirit who when brought
> Among the real tasks of life, hath wrought
> Upon the plan that pleased his boyish thought ;"

who has kept his first love, and striven for the chivalrous ideal of his youth ; who has loved truth and goodness with a passion so intense that they have become in him a new force, subduing, constraining, sanctifying the world about him; who for his very devotion to truth has dared to face doubts, for his very faith has dared to examine what he believes, "more brave for this, that he hath much to love ;" who from that familiarity with struggle and suffering which make other souls abate their feeling, has drawn a more compassionate tenderness; who, if he be called to mix in party strife, is able to "turn his necessity to glorious gain," winning modesty from the very temptation to self-assertion, large-hearted sympathies from the very contact of narrowness ; who in the heat of conflict never loses "the law in calmness made," in the tumult of voices yet hears, and reverences as king, his own conscience; who never used a base weapon, never drew sword in his own cause; who, because a life of conflict tends to bind his thoughts to earth, to make outward energy the substitute for depth of saintly devotion, lives therefore most in heaven, learns the lesson of quietness and confidence at Jesus' feet.

Brethren, have we not seen or known of such characters, such great and gentle souls? If so, we have seen the whole of the Apostle's mind. He does not call us to a philosophic indifference, nor to a dream of selfish asceticism. He would have us resist evil unto blood. He would that every base and cowardly thing done in our sight should go home as the stab of a dagger to our hearts. He would doubtless have us rebuke vice boldly, and refute error uncompromisingly, as he did himself. But yet he shews us a more excellent way: "Overcome evil with good." It is a lesson for our polemics. But surely it is also a suggestion of comfort and of strength. He who strives most to maintain the conflict against the evil of the world must feel most often the weakness of human weapons. It is a small and scattered band that seems at any particular moment to be waging war against established ill, and those who fight in it know best the feeble arms and half-traitorous hearts that are to be found in its ranks. And what a serried phalanx seems to be arrayed against them! not always the baseness only of the world, its interest and timidity and prejudice, but some too of its best and noblest, men of high self-devotion and pure and spotless lives. So it seems, but so it is not really. Look again in a little, and the mighty host is broken up, the ten have chased a thousand. What we had seen was but a shadow of the true combat.

Could our eyes have been opened, we should have seen that so far as our cause was really good, "those that were for us were more than those that were against us." That very nobleness of our opponents, which we may have thought our worst enemy, was in truth but the vanguard of our own army.

Good is not only the cause for which we strive, it is the very weapon of the strife itself. It is in itself aggressive; it is stronger than evil, and it draws men to itself by its own beauty and dignity. It is so in the world of thought and belief. Men do not love error, though they may be careless or obstinate. And it is so in the moral world also. Passion blinds men, the will fails, but they have not yet said "evil, be thou my good." They reverence good when they see it; if they saw it oftener they might be drawn closer to it. And so, brethren, in our strife with ill, whether it be false opinions, or evil practices, it matters more what we *are*, than what we *say*, or *do*. A truth that rules a character, goodness embodied in a noble and a gentle life, these are the powers that move the world. It is a fallacy to bid men perfect themselves before they try to reform the world about them, but it is not a fallacy to say that the two processes can only go on together.

So we are brought back to the government of our own hearts and lives, not as though the one duty of man were as modern paganism tells us, to develope each for himself his own nature as if it were a work of art; nor, as the religious counterpart of this view bids us, to save each for himself his own soul; but because there at least we can recognise and defy our Lord's enemy, because by conquering him there we are earning the right and the power to meet and conquer him upon a larger field.

What, then, are the weapons of our warfare at home in our own hearts? What other than those which in the world are "mighty to the pulling down of strongholds, to the bringing into captivity of every thought to the obedience of Christ."

"Overcome evil with good." Brethren, can we use these words and not feel how they describe God's dealings with us? Take them in the simplest sense of their original context, and how well do they pourtray even the God of natural religion, "the strong and patient Judge, provoked every day," who yet "leaves not Himself without witness in that He does good, and sends us rain from heaven, and fruitful seasons," how much more Him in whom we believe, who died for us when we were yet sinners, who came unto His own though they received Him not, who intercedes for those that crucify Him yet, and put Him to an open shame! And then, take the words in the larger sense in which we cannot doubt St. Paul intended them. They describe that characteristic of Christianity as a moral system which has lately been so eloquently set before us. It does not bind men by minute laws,—touch not, taste not, handle not,—but it inspires a motive which supersedes the need of law, a passion which can control all baser passions, can lift a man not only out of sin, but out of the desire and temptation of sin. Let us have the faith to apply that remedy to our own shortcomings which God has provided for the shortcomings of our nature. Good is a wide word, but it is not wider than the Apostle's precept. Let me bring down the principle to a few practical suggestions. Young men, you know each of you the plague of your own lives; you have resolved against it, you have striven against it, you have prayed against it. Have you tried to conquer it in the way which St. Paul advises? The evil spirit has not yet made his home with you, he comes only at intervals. Fill up the empty house against the time that he shall next return. Avoid bad companions by joining yourselves to good ones. Break down the bridge that connects you with your past follies. Throw your whole soul first into the plain duties of your daily calling, and then into all the healthy, bracing, manly interests which the life of young English citizens offers to you. You are *men;* think nothing that concerns humanity alien to you. Widen the circle of your thoughts. Force yourselves to take an interest in the great questions that are stirred, in the great subjects of knowledge that are opened, in the hopes and destinies of mankind that unfold themselves before you. Map out your time, and fill it up with work and with healthy amusements of mind and body. It is the empty listless mind that gives the sacred hours of leisure to day-dreams of folly, and suggestions of sin. It is the frivolous conversation that needs seasoning with hateful jests, and words that poison the memory.

Parents, do you too remember your responsibility in this matter. Remember that weeds grow apace in uncultivated ground, and the quicker for the goodness of the generous soil. Your sons may perhaps find wholesome interests and occupations elsewhere, but your daughters generally must find them at home, or nowhere. Do not leave them to seek their only relief from the tediousness of a flavourless home-life in foolish and mischievous novels, or still more foolish and mischievous gossip. Do not think that even religion by itself will supply the need. Such as the mind is, such is the religion. The religion of a trivial and selfish mind is trivial and selfish; it is only another and a sadder subject for gossip, another field for vanity and for malevolence. Give them a real interest in life, something which may raise their self-respect, which may freshen and give a tone to those tedious hours which after all make so large a part of most people's lives. We have not all high intellectual tastes, though we have far more than we usually gratify or even discover, but we all have hearts to feel for human nobleness and human suffering, and we all have, till it is stifled, a taste for simple and unselfish pleasures. Give them an interest in life; a care for something beyond the circle of their home and the details of daily life; an ideal that may lift and purify them. We come back to the old question,—How shall you implant such interest, or raise them to such an ideal, unless that interest and that ideal are your own? Enthusiasm is catching. One cannot live long with a friend of large heart and active charity without kindling, if it be but a spark, at his fire. But enthusiasm is not to be made to order.

Lastly, brethren, I have bidden you to apply to the evil of your own hearts the same *kind* of remedy as that which God has provided for the evil of our nature; may I not bid you apply the *very* remedy itself? Let us think how God has dealt with the sin of His rebellious creatures.

He has not been content to warn, to threaten, to set before them a strict and righteous law, which to break were death, but yet which all had broken; He has condescended to our weakness, He has given us not a law but an Example, not a perfect code but a perfect Man, not one who should say, "There is the path, walk ye in it," but One who says, "Come, follow Me."

And He has not only given us an *example*, He has found us a human *motive*. Few of us can rise to high abstract arguments, but few can feel that the good of the race or the perfection of their own nature is an adequate motive for self-denial. But all can feel love and gratitude to a person, all know that to deny themselves for one they love is a *pleasure*, not a pain.

Brethren, let us seek the inspiration of the Christian life, where apostles and martyrs found it, in the life and person of Christ. For His sake, and in His strength, let us fight our battle against sin, the world, and the devil ; *for His sake*, who loved us before we loved Him, in whom our fathers believed and were not confounded, who is very near us, who will never leave nor forsake us ; and *in His strength*, in the strength of His love, in the strength of His example, in the strength of those who know that they are following One who has all power in heaven and earth, who is ever with them, to uphold, to pardon, to crown them.

SERMON XI.

The Crisis of the Conflict.

ST. JOHN xvii. 3.

"And this is life eternal, that they might know Thee the only true God, and Jesus Christ, whom Thou hast sent."

THE intercessory prayer of our Lord for His disciples first, and then for His whole future Church, has ever been regarded by believers as one of the most precious passages of Holy Writ. Certainly it is one of the most solemn, and few we may hope can read this chapter without a sense of deep and heart-controlling awe stealing over them. It was spoken upon the evening preceding our Lord's passion, when now His earthly ministry was fast hastening to its close, and withdrawn from that world which had made His life a pathway of thorns, the Saviour gave His faithful followers His parting words of love and tenderness. They were spoken probably standing; "Arise," He had said, "and let us go hence." The paschal lamb had been eaten; the sacrament of the Saviour's broken body and blood, which was to take its place, had been instituted; the Psalms which ever followed that supper had been sung; the traitor had gone from their company upon his accursed errand: and left alone with the loving and the true, the Saviour spake to them as He had never spoken before; spake to them as friends, and gave them words of divine comfort. And they were

His last words to them till after His resurrection. When His prayer was over He went with them to the garden, and thence was hurried to the High Priest's hall, and the tribunal of the heathen governor, and to the cross. When the time came round again at which Christ had thus talked with them, His holy body, rent with the soldier's spear, lay in the rich man's tomb; and His soul was in the abode of the spirits of the dead. The true Paschal Lamb, whose blood can save from the destroying angel, had been sacrificed for the sins of mankind.

St. John does not expressly mention the institution of the Lord's Supper, which was to set forth that sacrifice to all generations of the faithful. The other three Evangelists had given so detailed an account of it, that all Christians fully knew every particular, and St. John seldom repeats again what they have told. But there is a constant reference to it in his narrative, as that which was to knit all believers together in the bond of love. He makes, however, a very significant addition to what we know of that eventful evening, for he alone tells us of Christ washing His disciples' feet. Strange that it should be so; for it was John's especial office to magnify his Lord. He it is who sets Him forth to us as the Word who was with God and was God; as the Bread whereof he that eateth shall never die; as the Water which springs up in the faithful to everlasting life; as the good Shepherd who lays down His life for the sheep; as the Way, the Truth, and the Life of His people; as the Vine who sustains them, and gives them their strength and sweetness. But while thus he magnifies Him, he also sets Him before us in this act of the deepest self-humiliation. The Lord of all lays aside His garments, and girds Himself with a towel, and as a slave washes His disciples' feet. Could love give a stronger proof of its earnestness? Could humility more plainly set the lesson of example? But was this all? The words to Peter, "If I wash thee not, thou hast no part with Me," tell us of a spiritual meaning to the act. Doubtless it symbolized the cleansing virtues of Christ's blood, of which the Christian daily stands in need; and withal reminds us how great was the humiliation of the Son of God, when He emptied Himself of His glory, and took upon Him the form of a servant that He might shed that blood whereby our sins are washed away.

Among those whose feet He washed was Judas Iscariot; and he, too, was partaker of His broken body, and of His poured out blood. But the presence of the traitor troubled our Lord; perhaps the thought saddened Him that so many in all ages would by their obduracy and hardness of heart make all His love unavailing; would join even in shewing forth His death, and yet crucify Him afresh by their sins. He grieved, too, for Judas himself. He had followed Him at first with the same professions of love as the rest, and had had committed to his charge whatever of earthly means the Saviour and His followers possessed; but he loved the world more than he loved his Master, and was plotting to deliver Him to His enemies. Jesus, therefore, was troubled in spirit, and testified that one of them should betray Him; and having pointed out who it was, as if eager to be free from the pollution of his presence, He sent him away. "That thou doest do quickly." He then having received "the sop, went immediately out; and it was night."

Night to Judas: he went forth into the outer darkness, but behind him he left light. For there was the

Saviour, who is the Light of the world, and now there were with Him only those who truly loved Him. They were still frail and erring: not long, and all for the time forsook Him and fled. But it was but human infirmity, and soon they gathered round Him again, and learnt from His cross the martyr spirit. As to loving and true friends, therefore, He spake to them, and His heart seemed as it were to overflow with thoughts, too deep even now, after men have for eighteen centuries meditated upon them, for us fully to comprehend them. For these last words of Christ refer almost exclusively to the profounder mysteries of the faith.

It is of the relation of God the Son to God the Father, and God the Holy Ghost, that the Saviour speaks; it is of His own mystical union with His people, and of their oneness with Him and with one another, and of the relation of His Church to the world. And as if feeling that neither His disciples then, nor believers afterwards, could easily attain to that spirituality which would enable them to understand these themes, He repeats again and again the most important principles of His discourse, as if He would rivet them on our memories; while He warns us, as He warned them, that it is only by the gift of the Holy Ghost that the Church can be led into all the truth. And the disciples as they clustered round Him listened in awe. They understood not as yet much of what He was saying; they knew not what great events would happen before the next night came round. But they knew that they were upon the very eve of great events. There was that in their Master's words which bade them be ready for scenes of danger. Like men in a trance, they moved forward from event to event, marking all that happened, with eyes open to observe, noting all in their memories; but not seeing the connection of events, understanding them not, knowing not what to do, or what to advise. This was the secret of their irresolution when the traitor and his band seized their Lord; it was as when in some great battle the general falls, and the army is paralyzed by his loss. The guiding mind which connected all their different movements and positions, and gave them unity, is no more; and they have become a crowd only, a multitude without a purpose. So with the Apostles, they understood not the purpose, the plan, the object of those events, in which they were taking part; and therefore their own wills were powerless. And no wonder. They were standing upon the dividing line between the Jewish and the Christian Church. The promises to which all believers hitherto had looked forward were now being fulfilled. It was the very crisis of the world's history; the battle of mankind lost by the first Adam in Paradise, was by the second Adam, as on that day, to be won upon Calvary. Yet a few hours, and the serpent would bruise the feet of the woman's Seed; but in the struggle, the woman's Seed would crush Satan's head beneath the cross: and having achieved the victory, with loud voice would cry, "It is finished." The sacrifice has been offered, man is saved, and sins can be forgiven.

We, brethren, are preparing in this Lenten season for thoughtful meditation upon our Lord's sufferings. On Sunday next we begin that solemn course, in which chapter by chapter, gospel after gospel, we follow Him in all that He did or bore for us. And no portion of the Bible at such a time can be more fit for our study than these His own last words with His Apostles. But they belong only to those who are truly His. You notice yourselves how carefully in the fourteenth chapter, when Judas asked how our Lord would manifest Himself unto them, but not unto the world, it is told you, that it was not Iscariot. Our Lord could not so have spoken of the Christian's holiest relations with his Saviour and his God, had the traitor been present; and so before we can feel that these words belong to us, we must have the joyful hope that we are true branches of the Vine, true members of Christ's Church, waiting here for the return of Christ our risen Head, that He may take us with Him to those many mansions which He is preparing in His Father's House. But to such as are Christ's people in very truth, this their Lord's last prayer for His Church is beyond measure precious. For where shall we find more plain directions as to what we ought to pray for, and what we ought to endeavour to become? For here we read what were the wishes of Christ's own heart, what the petitions which He Himself offered to the Father for His people. Surely that which He prayed we might become, should be the aim of our lives—that which we too should pray for, and strive to attain to. And in that small portion of it especially chosen for our meditation this evening, we have no light matter set before us, but are told the very secret of eternal life : " This is life eternal, to know Thee the only true God, and Jesus Christ whom Thou hast sent."

Now in these words we must first observe that the word *know* is used by St. John in a very strong way. It does not mean with him what we call knowledge— the merely being acquainted with what has been said or written upon any subject, and understanding it. When he wrote his Gospel there was a heresy prevalent which put knowledge in the place of holiness. It was a strange system, chiefly drawn from oriental philosophy, and dealing very little with the practical duties of life, but trying rather to explain the method of creation, and whence evil was derived, and by what steps the soul could move upwards; and St. John repeatedly alludes to this heresy, and uses its terms, but always so as to correct its errors. And thus, as it made knowledge to be man's chief good, he shews us what true knowledge really is. It had dwelt in his memory how his Lord had used the word, and he had felt how in Christ is contained all that truth which men seek in vain in philosophy. He tells therefore how Christ had spoken of His Apostles *knowing* the truth; of those who do God's will *knowing* the doctrine; of His *knowing* His sheep, and of their *knowing* His voice; and of the Father *knowing* Him; and of His *knowing* the Father. Now this last phrase may help in explaining to us something of the Apostle's meaning: God the Father knows the Son, and the Son knows the Father, by reason of the Divine unity. They are partakers of the same nature, the same attributes, and so united that whatsoever the Father doeth, that doeth the Son likewise. And so, then, with the believer; to know God is the effect of being made like unto Him. Infinite as is the distance between God and man in nature, it is not so in the realm of grace. There they are brought near to one another; for the Christian's growth in grace is the gradual formation in him of Christ's image, and as bearing that image, and thereby becoming one with Christ, he is united also to God the Father: and thus St. Peter even speaks of Christians as being made partakers of the Divine nature. In Christ, therefore, the believer is brought near unto God. As in Him the two natures were united in one Person, so those who are engrafted into Him by a living faith, are admitted into union with God. To use St. Paul's words, "Now in Christ Jesus, ye who sometimes were far off, are made nigh by the blood of Christ." And upon this nighness follows the privilege which the Apostle proceeds to describe, that "through Christ we both," i.e. (both Jew and Gentile) "have access by one spirit unto the Father." It was a privilege which the Jew had ever possessed, as living under a covenant with God, which was a foreshadowing of the Christian Church, and therefore anticipated some of its blessings; but the Gentile world had been left to the dimness of natural religion, until Christ came.

It is, then, to this close relation between God and man which is now made possible by the blood of Christ, that the Saviour refers in speaking of His disciples as *knowing* the Father. Eternal life is to be found only in God, who is the sole source of life and light. Even the word used of Him in the Greek, "the true God," expresses this. It does not signify *true*, as of one speaking truth, or as one whose promises are true, but refers to the reality of His existence; and thus in the Creed we translate it by the word *very*, itself a Latin word signifying 'true,' but referring to the truth and reality of Christ's divine nature. Christ we affirm to be —Very God of Very God,—God really, truly, essentially, and substantially. And this is the word used here. Eternal life is to know the Father as the only very God.

And with this knowledge is joined the knowledge of Christ, because it is by Him only that we can know the Father. So St. Paul tells us, "Being justified by faith, we have peace with God through our Lord Jesus Christ, by whom also we have access unto this grace wherein we stand." It is not the God of nature to whom the Christian draws nigh. The attributes of the Deity which nature proves to us, are, as the same Apostle teaches us, His eternal power and Godhead. But in Jesus Christ we learn His love; learn the purposes of mercy for which we were created and placed upon this earth; learn, too, the means provided for our restoration to more than that first glory of human nature which Adam bore when he walked with God in Paradise.

But this is but a small part of the meaning of this clause of the text. It speaks of the person of our Saviour as co-ordinate with God the Father in being the object of that knowledge, the effect of which is eternal life. And yet there is a contrast between the Saviour and the Father, who is described as the only very God. For the revelation of God in Christ Jesus is made to us, not by the Godhead of the Son, but by the union of the human nature with the Divine in His one person. And thus St. John says, "No man hath seen God at any time: the only-begotten Son, which is in the bosom of the Father, He hath declared Him." But how? Because "the Word was made flesh, and dwelt among us, full of grace and truth; and we beheld His glory, the glory as of the Only-begotten of the Father." Even more plainly St. Paul describes this office of our Lord, where he says to Timothy, "There is one God, and one Mediator between God and men, the man Christ Jesus." The text, therefore, teaches us that this saving knowledge of God is possible only by a knowledge of Jesus Christ as the revealer of God to mankind. God in His abstract essence man cannot know. The attributes which creation reveals to us fill us with wonder and awe, as we contemplate God's universal sovereignty, His infinite wisdom, His omnipotence. But however deep and true our feeling of the magnificence and beauty of God's works in creation, it produces no such spiritual effect upon the soul as to be in it a wellspring of eternal life. The Psalmist teaches us this, where, in the nineteenth Psalm, he contrasts the teaching of nature with that of revelation. "The heavens," he says, "declare the glory of God;" but it is "the law of God which is perfect, and converts the soul." We gaze in astonishment at God's handiwork in the firmament of heaven, but it is "the statutes of Jehovah which rejoice the heart and enlighten the eyes." And if David could so speak of old, when he had but types and shadows of the Saviour, how much more true must it be of us who have the substance! To know Jesus Christ, as sent by God, to know Him in those offices in which as the Mediator He brings us near to the Father, this is life eternal; and to this declaration of our Lord St. John in his Epistle refers, where he says, "This is the record, that God hath given to us eternal life, and this life is in His Son. He that hath the Son hath life, and he that hath not the Son of God hath not life."

Such, then, were the Saviour's last words to His Apostles, as they gathered round Him in awe during the few peaceful moments that remained before the agony in the garden. Already the shadow of the Passion was darkening upon Him, but He could not part from His loving followers without prayer for them. And in that prayer He told them the true nature of eternal life, that it consists in unity with the Son of God, whereby we know Him, and in Him God the Father. It is an awful theme, suiting the dread hour at which it was spoken; but St. Paul explains to us its meaning, such as we have set forth above, in his words to the Philippians, when he thus describes the struggle of his own life: "Yea, doubtless, I count all things but loss for the excellency of the *knowledge* of Christ Jesus my Lord, for whom I have suffered the loss of all things, and do count them but dung that I may win Christ, ... that I may *know* Him, and the power of His resurrection, and the fellowship of His sufferings, being made conformable unto His death, if by any means I might attain unto the resurrection of the dead."

Thus did St. Paul, though not present himself when Christ in His last prayer set forth before His Apostles the great object of His ministry, and of the office of the Church in all ages, yet shew how fully he had ever acted upon, and shaped his life by his Saviour's words. And by these words the Saviour still testifies to us what should be our great endeavour, and what it is which decides whether or not we belong to Him. In the lifelong struggle which, as the soldiers of Jesus Christ, we here maintain, that which wins for us the victory is the growing union with our Master wrought in the hearts of His believing people by His own gifts of grace. As we learn thus to know Him by growing like Him, we feel that we have passed from death unto life. If Christ be not formed in us, then, though we be outwardly members of the Church, it is only as Iscariot was in the company of the Apostles, and sooner or later the day will come when, as on the evening when Christ spake these words, the separation must be made between the false professor and the true believer. Up to this time Iscariot had walked with the Twelve; but he saw nothing in Christ but His human nature, and desired nothing from Him, but place, and power, and wealth, in a temporal kingdom. The other

Apostles, we know, had also shared these ambitious hopes : that very evening they had disputed who should be greatest. But they were gradually learning that there was more in Christ ; the feeling which Peter had once expressed, and which had stilled his doubts when many were abandoning their profession, " Lord, to whom shall we go ? Thou hast the words of eternal life ;" this love to Christ as the Giver of eternal life was fast overcoming all other feelings in their minds. That night, then, was the crisis of their lives. Hitherto they had followed our Lord with mixed motives, but now our Lord set forth before them His coming humiliation, and shame, and death; and that though for a short season they would see Him again, yet soon He would depart, and the Comforter who would come in His place, would be the Holy Spirit present in their hearts. He had long been preparing them for this, and now they must decide. Even after His words, which seem so plain to us, and after His long preparation, the crisis came upon them suddenly ; and at the first moment they failed. But the Eleven rose bravely from their fall, and from that day earth had lost its power over them. Their prayer now was to be made conformable to Christ's sufferings ; their eyes now were turned to Jesus as to one who had endured the cross for them, and despised the shame. Their happiness was to suffer. " I take pleasure," says St. Paul, " in infirmities, in reproaches, in necessities, in persecutions, in distresses, for Christ's sake."

So did they pass from death unto life; and their pathway is also ours. We, like them, have to choose between earth and heaven, between things temporal and things eternal. And that which gave them strength to win the victory must also strengthen us. We can never hope to overcome the world by our unaided efforts; it is possible only through Jesus Christ our Lord. Let us then, brethren, seek to know Him; let us seek it in prayer. In this very discourse He tells us, "Verily, verily, I say unto you, Whatsoever ye shall ask the Father in My Name, He will give it you." And as we pray, so let us try to live, endeavouring to follow our Saviour's example, seeking to become conformable to His death; so will earth lose its power over us, and spiritual blessings be more prized, and we shall daily more and more feel the truth of our Saviour's words, that life eternal is to be found in Him alone.

It is a noble hope that is set before us, to know Christ by growing like Him. It may seem almost more than we dare aspire to while we are still encompassed by the weakness of human nature. And yet we ought to aspire after nothing less; and, as if to encourage us, we see the Apostles failing in their first attempt. But how grandly did they arise from their fall! How different were those courageous men, who in the presence of the whole council said by the mouths of Peter and John, "Whether it be right in the sight of God, to hearken unto you more than unto God, judge ye," from the timid band who all forsook the Master whom they loved, and fled. But the reason is plain. In the intervening time they had passed the crisis. They had taken their side with Christ for ever. During the rest of their lives, good and evil, pleasure and pain, prosperity and adversity, were things judged of simply with reference to Christ. To know Him was their sole object of desire; and through evil report and good report they stedfastly "looked unto Jesus as the Author and Finisher of faith."

So with us. If we have taken our part finally with

Christ, we shall not fear lest the hope set before us be beyond our powers, and more than we dare aspire to. One thought will fill our hearts, one longing desire will animate our whole lives, the desire so to know Christ here as to dwell with Him for ever hereafter. And as thus we ever look to Him for help, for guidance, for instruction, for comfort, we gradually shall grow more like Him, and the beginning, the first preparation be made for that full perfection of which St. John speaks in those inspiring words, "We know that when Christ shall appear, we shall be like Him, for we shall see Him as He is."

We have examined then, brethren, the crisis in the lives of the Apostles; we have seen how they passed through it, and how faith won in them the victory. And what happened in them is recorded for our example. One caution, however, is needed. The crisis took place in them under the pressure of great events, and in a short space of time. Yet be sure that it only disclosed what had long been in preparation. Eleven of the Apostles had long been gradually drawing nearer Christ, one had been slowly separating from Him. Still they walked together, and except in small matters probably none marked the vast change which was surely growing up between them. But the events of the crucifixion suddenly brought it to light, and the one has throughout all ages since been held accursed as the traitor to his Lord, the rest have been reverenced as the founders of the Christian faith.

There may be those here who can look back to some one event in their lives as the turning-point, the dividing line in their own spiritual history. More, probably, cannot so look back. The Christian life has grown up so gradually within them, that like Samuel of old they have ever belonged to God from their first dedication to Him ; or they may still be altogether uncertain whether they belong to God or to the world. To these latter some crisis may come, some trial, or sore sickness, or other event which may disclose to them what they are. But what I would earnestly press upon you is, that the crisis does not make the difference, but only reveals it. Iscariot had long been growing conformed to the world before his betrayal of his Master proved it to himself and others. Peter long before had made his choice, when at a time of general unbelief he felt that Christ had the words of eternal life, and Christ alone. Depend upon it that in your daily ordinary actions, and in the common round of your usual duties you make your choice between life eternal in your Saviour, and death in the world. Strive, therefore, and pray that in your daily duties you may choose Christ. Strive in your allotted place and sphere to grow like Christ, and know His life-giving power ; then if the crisis come of some great and trying event, you will be yourselves surprised to feel how true your faith is ; and if no such event come, to disclose what you are to yourself, you will learn it even more certainly upon the morning of the Resurrection. But if you wait for some crisis to make you repent, and seek a Saviour, there are the boding words of Christ to warn you of your error, that those who hear not Moses and the prophets,—those, that is, for whom the Bible and the ordinary means of grace do not suffice,—such would not be converted though one rose from the dead.

SERMON XII.

The Great Overthrow.

PSALM ix. 6.

"O thou enemy, destructions are come to a perpetual end."

IN the vision of the Church in heaven, granted for the encouragement of the Church on earth, the victors in the strife in which we are engaged are described as singing "the song of Moses the servant of God, and of the Lamb." That is, they are described as keeping perpetual remembrance of the conflict they have endured. Their song is not of the future, but of the past. The host of the redeemed are pictured as looking back, like the host of Israel on the morning of their deliverance, over the troublesome waters through which their long night march has led them, and mingling with their triumph over the utter destruction of their enemy the memories of that night of weakness and weariness and fear. They sing the song of 'the servant of God,' the song of all good and faithful servants, no small portion of whose joy it will be to remember that good fight in which they were more than conquerors through Him that loved them. They sing 'the song of the Lamb.' By the power of sympathy they enter into the joy of their Lord—that deep joy He knew, when He, the true Moses, passed before His people alone through the depths of the grave and hell, and came forth leading captivity captive, destroying by His death him that had the power of death.

The whole history of the Church's pilgrimage here on earth, all the greatness and the mystery, all the weariness and the agony, all the patience and faith of her long warfare, as well as all the glory of her last crowning victory, all find their utterance in the song of Moses and the Lamb.

In that song it is our privilege even now to join. As it will be the joy of the Church triumphant to remember the trials of the Church militant, so it should be the joy of the Church militant to anticipate the rest and the peace of the Church triumphant. By faith the Church, while yet on earth, can ascend and dwell in heavenly places with her risen Lord; can see her warfare accomplished, her enemy vanquished; can take up her song of victory over him, and say now, even in the hour of her sorest and weariest strife, what she shall yet say in the hour of her final triumph, "O thou enemy, destructions are come to a perpetual end."

It is this sure and certain hope of the future that gives so peculiar a character both to the prophecy and the history of Scripture. It turns its prophecy to history. The prophet, as in this Psalm, sees the future so certainly accomplished, that he speaks of it as already passed; he does not say, thus and thus it shall be, but thus it is, thus it has been. And on the other hand, this certainty turns sacred history into prophecy. The narrator of some partial victory, some local triumph of God's people or judgment on God's enemies, exults over it in strains of praise that take, ere he is aware, a louder and a deeper tone than fits the occasion, and swell into the notes of the last great song of the Church triumphant: he sings the song of Moses and of the Lamb.

And it is in this spirit that the Church of Christ

should ever seek to interpret all history; not merely all Scripture history, where the conflict between good and evil is distinctly traced, but all history whatever. The history of our own hearts where flesh and spirit wage such deadly war; the history of the Church of Christ, from the first proclamation of enmity between the seed of the woman and the serpent, down to the last good word spoken or brave deed done for Christ, that proves the Captain of our salvation with us still; the history of the kingdoms of the world, with all its strangely intermingled good and evil, its terrible preponderance and triumph of evil over good; in all these, through all these, one thought should still be present with us, one clear, assured conviction sustain and guide us still,—the end of all this is fixed, certain, appointed from everlasting; evil shall be cast out of our world, good shall triumph in it everywhere and for ever; the destructions of the enemy shall come to a perpetual end.

It is of this assured certainty, it is of this ever-present vision of the final overthrow of all evil, which God has given to His Church, I have to speak.

I. And firstly, I would remind you *that this certainty is God's gift to His Church, and to His Church alone.* The final overthrow of all evil is a truth of pure revelation. From the written Word of God, and from it alone, do we learn the fact that the conflict between good and evil which we see and feel, is not eternal; that a time was when it was not, and a time is coming when it shall no longer be. We are too apt to forget this. Like other ideas which the Bible reveals to us, this idea of a final triumph has happily so leavened and possessed the minds of men, it seems so natural now to all of us to expect it, that we are really in danger of forgetting how entirely it rests upon the authority of revelation, how utterly impossible it is that it ever could have made a part of natural religion. So completely is this the case, that those who are most loudly calling on us to cast off our old superstitious belief in miraculous prophecy, are loudest in their prophecies of the final triumph of good, and the utter destruction of all evil. They are for ever assuring us of 'the good time that is coming,' when mankind shall have improved themselves by the aid of physical science, and political economy and natural morality, into universal virtue, wisdom, and peace.

But when turning away from this book which they bid us reject, we look upon those other revelations of God which still remain to us,—the natural world; human society; our own experience; all that we may call natural, as distinguished from supernatural,—what ground do we see of this hope? What voice of God in all these tells us that destructions are to have a perpetual end? Not the voice of nature; for that, ever interpreted more and more clearly by science, speaks of one great, awful, all-embracing law of vicarious suffering, by which the happiness, the progress of the race is purchased, by the suffering, the destruction of the individual;—the law by which the weak and the imperfect perish, that the strong may grow stronger and more perfect; the law by which the death or the agony of one sentient being, makes the life or the pleasure of another; the law by which an ever-wasting destruction is called in to check an ever-needlessly multiplying life;—laws which with one voice proclaim, that physical evil and pain must be as lasting as physical good, that suffering must still be the shadow of joy, and death still the condition of life, and that destructions shall never, can never come to an end.

Is it the constitution of human society, and the course of human history? More and more clearly are these revealing the working of that law of vicarious suffering, even in a more terrible form, the law by which the happiness of the few is dependent upon the suffering of the many. What is it that governs that high civilization of which we boast ourselves? The law which governs all human society, and which is the necessary condition of all civilization and progress, is the law of unequal distribution. All cannot have an equal share of wealth, and leisúre, and learning; all cannot be equally cultivated. An equal division would make all equally poor, not equally rich; it would arrest all progress. It is the law, then, of society, that many must be poor to allow of some being rich, many ignorant to allow of some being learned, many overworked to allow of some having leisure.

Civilization, then, and progress, mean just this—the refined, the graceful, peaceful lives of the few, purchased by the toil, the temptation, the weariness, the shortened, saddened lives of the many. Civilization has still, like all things human, its darker as well as its brighter side; its law of degradation, as well as its law of progress; and the one is still seen to be the necessary condition of the other. You may endeavour to lessen the pressure of this law, by enactments of human statesmanship, or the counteracting influences of Christian benevolence; you may lessen these inequalities, war against these evils, but you never can eradicate them.

And what is history, for the most part, but the record of the efforts men have been making to shift from one class or other of society the burthen of this law? What are the wisest or the wildest political movements, but attempts to adjust its pressure? None have ever perfectly succeeded: no social polity has ever been seen, so perfect as not to inflict some suffering or some wrong on some one class, none so lasting as not to need perpetual re-adjustment. There is a decay of institutions, as of men. New births there are, too, for these, but they are still preceded by the sickness and death of the old. Not gently and peaceably, but with convulsions and agonies does the old perish, and the new come to life. And here, too, this law seems eternal; these destructions seem to know no end.

Are we to look into our own hearts? Who ever there saw evil finally overthrown, good finally triumphant? Who ever could say, At last the warfare within me is over, and my will, in perfect accord with all the laws of right, rules absolutely and without effort all my nature? Who does not know that it is still the wisest and holiest of men who mourn most over the perpetual warfare they must wage against evil within them; how its destructions never cease, but threaten ever the wreck of their virtue and the ruin of their peace; how it compels for its conquest, the severest self-denial, the most ruthless sacrifice of many a joy and many even an innocent delight. And after all this lifelong struggle there awaits us, if in this life only we have hope, the undistinguishing grave, that involves in one common annihilation all alike;—the grave, beyond which the soul untaught of God can but send a guess or a wish, but never gains the vision of a sure and certain hope; the dark curtain, with its terrible inscription of "perhaps," that drops at last upon the stage of our conflict. Here is no assurance of the final overthrow of evil, not here do we learn that destructions come to a perpetual end.

Nor do we gain this assurance by resorting to a general belief in the goodness and benevolence of God, a persuasion that because He is good and loving, He must at last end all evil. For although creation does most largely testify to the goodness of God, yet it is clear that the idea of God's goodness creation gives us, can never rise beyond the amount of goodness revealed in creation. If that be, as it clearly is, a goodness which allows of evil,—nay, which has interwoven it in the whole plan of the universe,—how can we argue from the exhibition of such goodness, that evil is ever to be destroyed? If its existence is consistent with God's perfect law now, why not for ever? An instant of unnecessary evil or pain, is as inconceivable as an eternity of it; an instant of necessary evil seems to insure an eternity of it. And, therefore, if we are to judge of the purposes of God only by what He has done, and is doing in creation; if we are to judge of the future of the world only by the past, or the present, we must believe in the eternity of evil. The stream can rise no higher than its source. A natural religion can never rise above the teachings of nature, and if these declare one fact more clearly and uniformly than another, it is that evil, whether moral or physical, is natural,—is an inherent, essential, inseparable element in all forms of creature life; and that to talk of final deliverance from it is not to believe, but to contradict the Bible of nature.

No, the word which tells us of the deliverance of nature from what seems an essential part of nature, must be supernatural. Nature can tell us nothing of her future, for she can tell us nothing of her beginning. It must be another voice than hers that gives us a Genesis and a Revelation. If we would know this, we must listen in the spirit to the voice from heaven, which calls to us, as we seek hopelessly and wearily amidst the desolate places of earth for a sign that desolation shall have an end; or, in its pleasant places, for a promise that joy shall endure: "Come up hither, and I will shew thee things to come." "Ascend up above the region of nature, that thou mayest learn the true aim and destiny of nature;" and the voice that calls to us, is the voice which in the beginning said, "Let us make heaven and earth."

That voice it is, and that alone, which tells us that in the beginning evil was not; that there was a time when all was very good.

That voice alone can tell us that evil is not God's work, formed no part of the original constitution of things; that it was no imperfection in the material which He found to His hand, and which imposed itself upon Him as an indispensable necessity in all His work, but that it was a foreign element introduced into this world of ours, at least, from without; introduced by the evil will and power of a being, not of this world, and, therefore, which may be removed by a higher will, and by a mightier power. It is God who tells us, and He alone can tell us, "an enemy hath done this."

But He tells us more than this. The knowledge that an enemy hath introduced evil into this world gives us no certainty it shall ever be cast out; for, as we have seen, if God Almighty could for a moment permit the existence of evil here, we have no right to say that He could not permit it always. The reason for His tolerance of it, for aught we can tell, might be eternal, and so too would be the evil. We need, for the certainty of its end, another revelation; we need, not only that God should say an enemy hath done this, but that He should say, the destructions of that enemy shall come to an end. And this is the revelation He has given us. He has given it, not only in the express words of those prophecies which from the first foretell this end, and which fix, though in mystic dates and figures, the very date of this end. But He has given us a still more certain assurance. To the word of His prophets He has added a sign. He has shewn us evil already overthrown, our great enemy completely vanquished. This Book reveals just that one fact of which all nature supplies no single instance, one case, not of partial and temporary, but of complete and final victory over evil.

Our Gospel, our good news for man, is this, that humanity, represented in its great Head and Chief, has encountered the Evil One, has foiled his temptation, endured the worst his hatred can inflict, passed through his prison-house of death; has risen, has ascended to the heaven from which he has fallen, and dwells there for ever. The voice which speaks from heaven of the end yet to come, is His voice—the voice of Him who was dead, and is alive for evermore; of Him, whose promise to us is that, because He lives, we shall live also. The voice of Him, who, in the crisis of His great strife, saw the travail of His soul already accomplished; saw the world for which He died, given Him as His eternal inheritance, purchased with His Blood; saw the glorious future of that reign which must continue till all things are put under His feet; and seeing it, exclaimed, "It is finished!" That word of His it is our right to repeat. In the life, death, resurrection, and ascension of Christ, we see the pledge of the resurrection, of the ascension of humanity beyond the reach of the Evil One; we see the works of the Devil destroyed by the manifestation of the Son of Man; we say, "It is finished." "O thou enemy, destructions are come to a perpetual end."

Viewed in the light of this revelation, nature, that before could tell us nothing of the end, now gives us a mighty assurance of it. For every proof she gives of this enmity of the destroyer, becomes a pledge of his destruction. The more pitiless the havoc, the wider the desolation he has wrought, the deeper grows our conviction that our Almighty and all-loving Father will not, cannot leave the enemy to work this cruel havoc, an instant beyond that time which He has set wherein to work by evil a greater good. The remainder of the wrath must be restrained, and restrained for ever. And thus, as we look upon each scene of ruin that tells the destroyer has been there, it tells us that the restorer is yet to come. The once pleasant places, the gardens of our delight that he makes desolate, foretell by their very barrenness the hour when they shall blossom as the rose. The fenced cities of our joy that he lays into ruinous heaps, proclaim the hour when they shall be replaced by the city of God, the heavenly Jerusalem, through whose gates no evil thing shall ever enter. The thirst of our souls, fevered by the poisonous wounds he has inflicted, foretells the cool and refreshing streams of the water of life, beside whose banks grows the Tree whose leaves are for the healing of the nations. The very pains of creation become prophecies of rest: it groans, but it groans in travail; it travaileth with the birth of the new creation, where destructions shall be unknown for ever.

And so the old word of triumph of the warrior becomes ours, " Out of the eater comes forth meat, out of the strong sweetness." We raise against our enemy our song of triumph, though we sing it with quivering lips; and by the anguish with which they quiver, and the sorrow that chokes our speech, we know that the morning of joy shall succeed the night of weeping, and we exclaim, "O thou enemy," because of the deadliness of thine enmity, because of the cruel ingenuity of thy torture, because of the fierceness and pitilessness of thy wrath, we know that "destructions shall come"—aye, we can say in assured faith, are come—"to an end" for ever!

II. In the next place we observe that, *while the date of this overthrow is concealed, the manner of it is largely revealed.*

The date of it is concealed. "Of that day or hour knoweth no man," because such knowledge would be hurtful to the Church; hurtful in her earlier days, by shewing her deliverance so far off that faith and patience would have been too sorely tried; hurtful in her latter days by bringing that hope so near that her faith and patience would have scarcely any trial at all; and mischievous, therefore, at any time to seek for and guess at. No spirit is more injurious to the real, earnest, patient Christian life than a spirit of eager, impatient curiosity, which is for ever peeping and prying behind the veil which God has interposed between us and the future; writing perpetual supplements to the Apocalypse; announcing, with all the solemnity and precision of a herald, the very day when the great procession of judgment is to appear, and assigning to each personage his exact place in it: announcements which the course of events is sure to contradict, and which the author must forthwith replace by new ones, given with just as much confidence as if the old had not just proved a failure.

We say nothing of the mischief that such Christian

soothsaying does to those without by the ridicule which it casts upon the awful themes which it profanes; but we would earnestly impress on you the mischief it does within the Church; the spiritual dissipation, the love of excitement, the distaste for sober, practical study of God's Word, that it is sure to generate. We only remind both those who indulge in it, and those who, because of it, scoff at prophetical studies, that for such sensational treatment of prophecy Scripture gives no warrant, and against it, it gives more than one express and solemn warning.

But just as it is not good for us to know or to guess at the precise date of the end, so it is good for us to know and meditate on the manner of it; and therefore He who will not tell us the time of the end, does tell us that concerning the manner of it that is calculated to help, and not to hinder, our Christian life meanwhile.

Two things He more especially tells us. Firstly, that it will not be brought about by the gradual wasting away of evil, and the gradual growth and spread of good; that we are not to look to see our present Christendom gradually conquering all heathendom, and growing the while more and more perfect and Christ-like. On this point our Lord's words seem decisive, making His coming in judgment to Jerusalem the type of His last final coming to judge the world. He tells us how that coming is to be preceded, not only by manifestations of the power of evil in the world of nature, by wars and famines and earthquakes, but by manifestations of its power within the Church, of which those outward ills are but the shadow; by apostacy and false prophets, by wide-spreading heresies, by waxing iniquity and waning love, by the dying out of living faith from the earth, until the carcases—the dead forms of dead religions and churches—lie waiting and inviting the gathering of the vultures of judgment to cleanse the earth of them for ever.

So St. Paul foretells the "falling away" first, "the revelation of the man of sin," "to be destroyed only with the brightness of the Lord's coming;" so in the vision of St. John the shadows grow darker and the lights fainter as the vision draws to a close. The forms that rise up out of the abyss grow more bestial and horrible. So the beast succeeds the dragon, and the mouth of the beast speaks still fiercer blasphemies, and Babylon the great grows still mightier, and she, whose name is Mystery, drinks deep, even to drunkenness, of the blood of the saints, and the witnesses lie slain in the streets of the great city, and the woman flies into the wilderness; until at last heaven is opened, and He, who is faithful and true, comes forth to judge and to make war in righteousness, and to win His great victory that proclaims Him King of kings, and Lord of lords.

Of the meaning of all the details of these mystical pictures there may be, and there is, great debate and doubt; but surely no doubt of this much at least, that they all foreshadow, not a great growth of good and decay of evil, but rather a great growth of evil and decay of good, to be ended at last by a sudden final overthrow of evil at the coming of the Lord.

It is good for us to remember this. It preserves us from a false estimate of the Church's mission in this dispensation. The Church must be known by her work, but we must take care we understand what that work is, or we shall be unreasonably expecting that from her which she was not sent to do. Her work is warfare against evil everywhere, complete conquest over evil nowhere. Not by the completeness of her conquest over evil, but of her antagonism to all evil, are we to judge how far she is true to her mission. To look for more than this is sure to lead to disappointment, perhaps to unbelief; to look for less than this is sure to lead to carelessness and sloth. To look only for this; to understand that we are to contend against every possible form of evil, and yet that we shall never succeed, in this dispensation, in casting out any one form of evil; to work as if all were to be done by us, to wait as if nothing were to be done by us; to know that the warfare is still to be ours, and the victory at last, not ours, but our Lord's; this is "the patience and the faith of the saints."

2. Again we learn another truth concerning the manner of this overthrow, and that is, that it will be visibly and unmistakeably miraculous, that it will be seen to be of such a nature as to be solely and exclusively God's work, and not in any way man's work, nor yet the result merely of an increase of what we call the ordinary workings of His Spirit amongst us; but rather such a manifestation of the Divine power in the person of Christ as shall bring out distinctly before us all the true character of this great conflict, that it is a strife, not of force, or of laws, but of wills, of persons; a war, not of *good* against *evil*, as we might imagine it to be now, but of the *Evil One* against God and *His Christ*.

Of the nature of the signs that usher in that last great convulsion there may be doubt and debate. How far all those physical signs and wonders in the heaven and the earth that are to accompany it,—the darkening sun and the waning moon, and the falling stars, and the heavens shrinking as a scroll,—how far these are to be

regarded as strictly literal, how far symbolical, the end
alone will tell; but of the general purport of them, so
far at least there can be no doubt, that such signs and
tokens shall accompany it as shall prove it to be the
work, not of nature or natural forces, but of nature's
God. Whatever other sign shall be revealed, one shall
be seen above all, the sign of the Son of Man in
heaven. The power that destroys all evil, the great
glory that restores all good, shall be seen to be His,
and His alone.

And it is well for the Church that she does possess
this prophecy of the manner of the end. It helps to
keep alive her faith in God; her faith, that is, in God in
the only sense in which the word God has any religious
meaning; her faith in a will—not a first cause, a per-
vading force, but a supreme, all-ruling, all-ordaining
personal will, in which we can trust, to which we can
pray—a will, the thought of which delivers us from
the awful tyranny of soulless, unintelligent, mechanical
law. And it is this faith, the very ground of all religion, that needs in these latter days to be strengthened
against the ever-growing idolatry of law, which threat-
ens to supersede the worship of the lawgiver; that
worship of the creature rather than of the Creator which
in one form or other has been the world's great temptation to the Church: a temptation which is seducing
Christian men not only to misinterpret the phenomena
of the natural world, but even those of the spiritual
world, the kingdom of grace: a temptation to narrow
as far as possible the limits of the supernatural, and to
enlarge as much as possible the limits of the natural;
to shew in how very low and merely natural a sense
we may say, the Bible is God's word to man, prayer is
man's speech to God, or the sacraments God's gift of

supernatural grace; to shew how all these doctrines may be made ingeniously to fit in with a system of laws and forces which may be seen and measured and weighed and calculated; to explain away, in short, God out of the Bible and the Sacraments and the Church, because it is the fashion now to explain Him away out of the world.

Now against this idolatry of nature—against this dread and dislike of the supernatural even in the kingdom of God—this temptation to subordinate the Church, whose laws are supernatural, to the world, whose laws are natural, and to make the constitution of the physical and material the rule by which to interpret the constitution of the spiritual,—against this, God has armed His Church by revealing to her the great antagonistic truth that it is not the world whose natural history conditions and limits the history of the Church, but the Church whose supernatural history shapes and rules the history of the world; that the destiny of man is not to be learned by investigating the laws of nature, but the destiny of the world to be learned by a knowledge of the true history of man. He reveals this to us first, in that great supernatural fact—the central fact of the world's and of the Church's history—the Incarnation; reveals to us in it the transcendent importance of that human history, in the course of which God became man; shews how the whole world—nay, if needs were, the whole universe—were fitly regarded but as the temporary platform on which this great fact were wrought out; how all its history, from all that infinity of ages science tells us of, were sufficiently accounted for, if it existed for this only; how its utter annihilation were but a small matter compared to the loss of one soul for which Christ died.

He shews us, too, how the whole of that history of man, which thus dominates the history of the world, is altogether supernatural. That it is in some degree unnatural we have already seen. It is unnatural that the evil will of an enemy should introduce disorder into God's order, lawlessness into His law. It is unnatural that man's will should continue in rebellion against the will of his Creator. But it is a supernatural thing that the Divine will should suspend the operation of that great natural law by which death should instantly have followed sin, that Omnipotence should hold apart for a time acts and their true consequences, crime and punishment, desert and reward. Not judgment inflicted but judgment delayed, not goodness triumphant but goodness suffering, not right and might miraculously united for ever, but right and might miraculously separated even for one moment,—this is the real miracle, the great mystery of mysteries.

This is the word of history; and the word of prophecy is like unto it. As history reveals to us disorder unnaturally introduced and supernaturally restrained, so prophecy reveals to us order supernaturally restored; shews us that Divine will which now overrules evil, appearing to overthrow it; shews us the true, the natural moral order of the world restored, the law of righteous government working the true unity between right and might, purity and joy, on the one hand, and between wrong and weakness, wickedness and death on the other; shews the whole history of our race on earth to be one long supernatural pause and parenthesis in a far vaster history, whose deeper laws and mightier forces embrace and girdle in from the first our lawless unrest.

And these two great lessons mutually strengthen

each other. Believe in the will that supernaturally overrules, and you have less difficulty in believing in the will that shall supernaturally overthrow evil. Believe in the will that is supernaturally to overthrow evil, and you will have less difficulty in believing in a will that is controlling and overruling it now.

III. And now of the result of that great overthrow of the new heavens and new earth which is to come forth at God's command from the ruins of the old, what have we to say? But little, for God has told us but little. It doth not yet appear what we shall be. It could not yet appear. The mortal cannot comprehend immortality, the corruptible incorruption. The language which foretells these becomes mystic and symbolical. The city whose gates are precious stones and whose streets are gold, that needs not the light of the sun, or the moon, through whose streets flows a mystic river, by whose banks grows a mystic tree of life,—what does it tell us, save that the language which men speak on earth has no words in which it were possible to reveal the joys of heaven? Nay, even those words which seem most intelligible, those which tell us rather what we shall *not* be, than what we shall be,—that there shall be no sin, nought that defileth, no curse; how sorrow and sighing shall flee away, and God Himself wipe away all tears from all eyes,—even these, when we ponder on them, seem full of mystery; for with the vanishing away of all that is evil, it seems to us as if there must also vanish much that is good. There are many of the noblest elements of goodness that seem impossible, save as existing in antagonism to evil. To say there shall be no evil in the world, seems to be equivalent to saying, there shall be no pity, no mercy, no benevolence, no fortitude, no courage, no self-sacrifice; that is, it seems to say that, though this life be our preparation for another, yet that some of the very chief of those lessons we shall have learned here, shall be useless there.

All this may serve to shew us that a condition of pure and unmixed good, of which we talk so freely, is really quite as inconceivable, perhaps more so than one of unmixed evil; and that heaven is quite as great a mystery as hell.

One thought, however, we can with some distinctness grasp; it is the one suggested in our text. It is this, that it must be a state of infinite progress; a life, not, as we too often think of it, of progress arrested, a life in which humanity, at once perfected, has before it only an eternity of virtuous repose; but a life of intense and glorious activity. The promise of eternal life necessarily implies this, for life is something more than existence. Life, in its truest meaning, is the highest and happiest manner of being; it is existence with every faculty, every power of our nature in its fullest, freest exercise. Whatever falls short of this, whatever checks or limits any one faculty, whatever of weariness or weakness there be in us, comes from the imperfection of our life, comes from its invasion in some measure by its antagonist death. And so we call it "this mortal life." This life, whose every breath, whose every movement, is one half death,—for such a life rest is essential, because the destruction of it is incessant. But the very idea of perfect life, a life that knows no strife with death, that needs to defend itself against no destruction, to repair no waste, implies, not eternal repose, but eternal activity, the life of a spiritual, intelligent, immortal creature, whose whole being, whose every power and faculty lives, intensely lives, in the glorious activity in which perpetual service and perpetual rest are one. "They rest, saith the Spirit, from their labours." And yet "they cease not day or night," proclaiming by all the unwearied actings of their glorified natures, saying, with the eternal hymn of an eternally happy life, "Glory, and honour, and power, be unto the Lamb for ever!"

For such a race there must be eternal progress, for there must be eternal acquisition without the slightest loss. How much of our life is lost in our perpetual warfare against death! How much in the labour for the meat that perisheth! How much in those low, wearing, petty cares and anxieties that weigh down to earth the noblest souls! How much of each life, how much of the sum of all lives, seems wasted in our mere effort to live! And, then, for the whole race in any one age, what hindrances, what interruptions to its progress in these destructions of the enemy! How much of the experience of each life perishes with it! What glorious treasures of knowledge are buried in each generation over and over again! What long, long ebbings of the tide of progress, what irregularities and uncertainties in its flow! What precious things it carries and sweeps away! How small a portion does each generation inherit of the wealth of its predecessor, and how little does it leave to that which succeeds it!

This is the great destruction of our enemy. A mortal race can never be a perfect race. But think of the infinite progress, in glory and honour, of the race that possesses immortality; a race, each individual of which is for ever contributing, to the common inheritance of knowledge and happiness, the imperishable gifts of a spirit made perfect! Think of the eternity of a race to whose progress there is actually no limit, save that which forbids the finite to become infinite, which leaves therefore to the creature, who still adores and contemplates and approaches to his Creator, still an eternity of progress!

And this is the hope set before us in the Gospel: the "inheritance incorruptible, undefiled, that fadeth not away," of which nature gives no promise, science no prophecy, history no hope; the inheritance which the miracle of redemption has purchased, and the miracle of revelation made known, and the miracle of regeneration conveys. These are the good things which God hath hidden from the wise and prudent,—too wise to believe in the invisible, too prudent to trust in the undemonstrated,—but which He hath revealed to babes, to loving, trusting hearts whose highest wisdom is to know their Father's voice, and whose deepest prudence is to trust their Father's word. To these, and these alone, it is given here to sing this song of triumph and joy; they, and they alone, can say "O thou enemy, destructions are come to a perpetual end!"

The song that shall fully utter all that hope implies, cannot be sung on earth; it is that "new song" which those whose pilgrimage is still unaccomplished, whose warfare is yet unended, cannot yet learn. Nay, even that song of victory whose notes we have been trying to catch to-night, we cannot often sing. It is our war-song here; we sing it at times as we enter into the battle; but in the strife the song of triumph is replaced by the sigh of weariness, and the groan of pain, and the cry of warning. Into that strife each one of us, who lives for God, enters as he leaves this place. The long narrow path through the troublesome waters stretches out before us again; and for the safe shore, and the bright morning, and the overthrown enemy, we see only the next step before us, and that but dimly often, and the clouds of doubt and perplexity above us, and behind us is the voice of the pursuing enemy, and our hearts grow faint and our feet weary, as we pass on slowly, uncertainly, fearfully, often, no song of praise upon our lips, happy if we are always able to speak the needful prayer for help. Aye, and sadder than this, we find it hard to remember that we are pilgrims at all. The vision of glory grows dim, the song of victory faint, not only in the night of spiritual trial and the weariness of spiritual warfare, but in the broad glare of the working-day world and the noise of the great battle of life.

Let us bear away with us, then, as helps, to be availed of at some future moment of temptation, these two truths that we have been contemplating. Against this overmastering tyranny of the visible which ever wars against the power of the invisible, the thought of the awful, the truly supernatural character of this present life, the terrible strife of wills, in which our wills are taking part, in a world in which Satan contends with Christ for the souls of men. Against the weariness and faintheartedness that feels the reality and the greatness of this life, but feels too its weariness and its risk, the thought of the assured and promised victory revealed in the Church's song of triumph, "O thou enemy, destructions are come to a perpetual end."

Printed by James Parker and Co., Crown-yard, Oxford.

www.ingramcontent.com/pod-product-compliance
Lightning Source LLC
Chambersburg PA
CBHW032143160426
43197CB00008B/759